The
Devon
gardens
guide

by

Rosemary Lauder

With a Foreword by
Michael Hickson
Vice-President, Devon Gardens Trust

Alison Hodge

First published in 2004 by
Alison Hodge
Bosulval, Newmill, Penzance, Cornwall TR20 8XA
info@alison-hodge.co.uk www.alison-hodge.co.uk

ISBN 0 906720 34 6

British Library Cataloguing-in-Publication Data
A catalogue record for this book is available from the
British Library.

Designed by Christopher Laughton
Edited by Edward Cheese
Originated by BDP – Book Development & Production,
Penzance, Cornwall
Printed in Spain

Contents

There is probably no area in the world where such a wide variety of plants can be grown as in the south-west of England. Horticulturally, the county of Devon has a proud heritage: its diverse topography and climate have not only created a challenge for the gardener, but have also provided a haven for the important collections of plants in the county.

Devon has many beautiful and unusual gardens. The sun-blessed slopes and estuaries inland from the south coast are probably among the sunniest sites in the British Isles, providing ideal conditions for the sub-tropical flora found here. In contrast, the harsh northern coastline, with its high granite cliffs, helps to protect the many wooded coombs and garden treasures from the salt-laden winds borne inland by the Atlantic storms. The south-facing estuaries, and associated farmland areas, are of a rich red earth, very different from the poorer, dull-coloured soils that can be flecked with stone (shillet) in the north. The vast moorland area of Dartmoor (over 600m/2,000ft high),

Foreword by Michael Hickson, Vice-President, Devon Gardens Trust

along with the western slopes of Exmoor (500m/1,640ft high), are National Parks with different soil types of a peaty nature. These are all ideal habitats for virtually every variety of hardy or nearly hardy plant once they are acclimatized.

The pattern of rainfall is variable across the county, from 60cm (23in) along the south coast, to 210cm (82in) on the moors. These areas attract the moisture-laden westerly winds. Long, clear, fast-flowing rivers emanate from among the tors to radiate out through the wooded valleys to the sea. Many of the inland gardens follow these winding valleys, to include some most wonderful views and cultivated plants within their design. Unfortunately, these valleys can be frost pockets, with plants often being subjected to frosts in late May, defying the description of Devon as a mild county.

The rich native flora has been a helpful guide to what can be grown by the plant enthusiast. As a result, the gardens of Devon are rich and diverse, with plant species introduced from the mild temperate, and even sub-tropical, zones of the world. The natural landscape also affords the perfect setting for designing gardens, in such a way as to encourage rare, and even endangered species that have specific needs, and require care and cosseting by their dedicated owners. Each of these gardens, whether great or small, harbours its own particular style.

In *The Devon Gardens Guide*, Rosemary Lauder has admirably drawn together the many different gardens from within the county, with the purpose of encouraging visitors to them. There is a potted history for each property, telling us briefly, where appropriate, about the house, the family, and how the garden we see today came into being. With the aid of this very informative gazetteer, it is possible to plan visits to the gardens of Devon throughout the year. As it should be, the brief descriptions of plants make this a tantalizing book for plant enthusiasts, encouraging them and everyone else to visit the gardens described. For however much of a plant enthusiast you may be, gardens, with their own special surprises, can be of joy and interest to us all.

Michael Hickson
Vice-President, Devon Gardens Trust,
formerly Head Gardener at Knightshayes

The Devon Gardens Guide is the most comprehensive guide to the gardens of Devon. It includes more than 100 private gardens, and public parks that open regularly, and a supplementary list of 24 gardens that open occasionally, or are gardens that have opened to the public only recently.

For each garden in the main gazetteer, there are map references, road directions, and full details for enquiries. Typical opening times and facilities are listed. English Heritage gradings in their *Register of Parks and Gardens*, and their *Register of Buildings*, as well as national and local designations for landscape beauty are included, to indicate those places officially recognized – although this in no way suggests that many other gardens are not equally, and in some cases more worth visiting.

Practical gardeners will welcome the notes for each of the main gardens on size, altitude, aspect, average rainfall and temperature, and soil – each of which affects the growth of plants.

The Guide is lavishly illustrated with photographs of the location and special features of the gardens, and specimens of individual flowers, many of which are characteristic of the local climate. The Introduction looks briefly at the geology and climate of the region; at the development of horticulture and design through the ages, in relation to Devon gardens, and particularly at the many public parks and gardens in the county.

Further information about the wealth of historic gardens in Devon may be found in *Devon Gardnes: A Historical Survey*[1], and in *The Garden History of Devon*[2]. Plant-

lovers are referred to W. Arnold-Forster's classic *Shrubs for the Milder Counties*[3], and Philip McMillan Browse's *Gardening on the Edge*[4], which describes present-day experiences.

Rosemary Lauder
March 2004

1 Devon Gardens Trust, 1994, *Devon Gardens: A Historical Survey*, Devon Gardens Trust.
2 Gray, T., 1995, *The Garden History of Devon: An Illustrated Guide to Sources*, University of Exeter Press.
3 Arnold-Forster, W., 2000, *Shrubs for the Milder Counties*, 2nd edn., Alison Hodge.
4 McMillan Browse, P., 2004, *Gardening on the Edge*, Alison Hodge.

Preface

Devon is an enormous county, the third largest in the country, covering 2,588 square miles (670,343 ha) of diverse countryside. It is nearly square, being some 75 miles (121km) at its longest, and 73 miles (117km) wide, bounded to north and south by the sea, and to the west by the mighty River Tamar, which marks the border with Cornwall. Only the eastern boundaries with Somerset and Dorset follow traditional rather than geographical lines. Much of the population is centred around Plymouth, Exeter, and Torbay, with huge empty spaces on the heights of Dartmoor. There are more miles of roads in Devon than in any other county, with a bewildering network of lanes leading to farmsteads, isolated hamlets, and remote manor houses.

Introduction

Much of the county, with its two long coastlines, is dominated by the sea, and this has a considerable influence on the climate. In the south, frost is a rare occurrence, and the warm, temperate climate enables a remarkable range of plants to flourish. On the north coast, although milder than inland, the strong winds wreak havoc, and only in the sheltered valleys is gardening possible. Further inland, north Devon has many fine gardens, but shelter is all important. The bulk of Dartmoor, rising in places to 610m (2,000ft), dominates the whole county, and is visible from all but the eastern areas. Some 77,700ha (300 square miles) of moorland, formed of ancient granite, it is a bleak and intimidating mass, where the winds cut all growing things, and the rain can seem relentless. (The highest level of rainfall – often over 252cm/100in annually – was recorded at Princetown.) Gardening under such conditions is all but impossible, but in the valleys and around the edges of the moor are some remarkable gardens, taking advantage of the high rainfall and the abundant water courses. It is from Dartmoor that all the rivers of south and west Devon flow.

The geology of the county consists of ancient granite, with old red sandstone to the west and south. The River Exe forms a rough dividing line between the older rocks of west Devon and the newer red rocks that stretch up into the Midlands. Culm measures overlie much of north and mid-Devon, and here there are large areas of poorly drained, stodgy soil of little agricultural value, but which are increasingly popular with the Forestry Commission. Limestone and newer sandstone forms the countryside of east Devon, with outcrops of red sandstone along the coast, fading beyond Seaton into the white cliffs of Beer. The county has a large variety of stone, and quarrying was once an important activity, the results of which are to be found in most parish churches, and larger farms and manor houses. Away from the creeping urbanization of the towns, with their business parks and shopping villages ringed with rushing traffic, the county is still peaceful and unspoilt: people still matter, and there is plenty of time for that most relaxing of pastimes – gardening.

Garden history

The early days

The earliest recorded gardens in Britain were those of the monasteries, much of what was grown behind their cloistered walls being for medicinal purposes. Before the dissolution of the monasteries in the time of Henry VIII, it was to the monks that people turned for healing and for teaching: monasteries were a great storehouse of knowledge. In one fell stroke Henry VIII erased centuries of history, and a whole culture that has never been replaced. It is hard to conjure up that lost world, which revolved around prayer and a rigid pattern of worship, unquestioned and seemingly unshakeable, but the loss of the monasteries must have been a tremendous blow to the local population.

No monastery gardens survive in Devon, but on the north coast, at **Hartland Abbey** (above; 24), parts of the original layout can still be seen, and something of the calm atmosphere still pervades this out-of-the-way haven. The development of the Abbey is well documented, from its days as a monastery, through its transformation to a manor house, and up until the present day. The medieval fishponds, many of the walls, and the

small stone bridges across the Abbey river are all survivals from monastic days. At **Buckland Abbey** (2), in west Devon, which passed to Sir Richard Grenville and later to Sir Francis Drake, much survives, including the tithe barn and many of the walled enclosures. The garden of the **Bishop's Palace** in Exeter is perhaps one of the oldest in the county, lying between the great wall of the cathedral and the Roman city wall, where some fine trees and an early orchard provide unexpected peace in the centre of the city.

The nobility of the county would also have had some form of garden for their enjoyment, but the provision of food was the more important. All manors of any size, and even quite modest farmhouses, had warrens for rabbits, fishponds, orchards, and herb gardens – all of which had a higher priority than flowers. These were found in 'my lady's garden', which was usually a sheltered enclosure where the ladies could enjoy the fresh air undisturbed. Those with sufficient land would have created a deer park, both for provision of meat and for sport. There were many such throughout the county, surviving up until the First World War in some cases, and the enclosing walls can

still be traced – as at Berry Pomeroy Castle, **Bicton** (53, 54), **Saltram** (10), King's Nympton Park, and **Powderham Castle** (47). This last remains not only complete, but well stocked with deer. The Courtenay family has always owned Powderham, and the beautiful parkland bordered by the Exe Estuary contains many fine trees, woodland, and a rose garden on the terrace.

Dartington Hall (above; 75) is among the earliest of Devon gardens to survive in recognizable form. Because the medieval manor, begun in about 1384 for King Richard II's half-brother, has had a peaceful history, the grounds have suffered less disturbance than has been the case elsewhere. The property passed down through country squires without the ambition or wealth to be fashionable, and thus we can still cross the 14th-century tilt-yard, with its terraces and columnar yews, and admire the long ranges of old stone buildings, including the marvellous medieval hall.

Gardens are transitory things, so quickly do they return to the wild once the hand of man is removed. A few decades of neglect, and all that will remain of a once-great garden will be some trees, traces of old walls, or a level area once the lawn, to give a clue that something else existed. Tantalizing remains have been found at Oldstone, Blackawton, ruined by a disastrous fire in 1893; and at Shilstone, near Ugborough, an early landscape garden has been rescued, and is in the course of restoration. Here the sheltered valley was overlooked by a walled enclosure with a gazebo. A stream runs through an intriguing stone chamber, issuing into a pool before being channelled into slate-lined rills, which course down the valley sides to a pond at the bottom.

The 18th century

Well-documented early gardens existed at Poltimore, outside Exeter; Heanton Satchville in mid-Devon; Buckland Filleigh nearby, and at **Castle Hill** (right; 15) in north Devon. These were all formal gardens in the grand manner, with long avenues of trees, lovely vistas, and much statuary, the overall design governed by formal straight lines. Very little of this style of garden survives in recognizable form, although at **Bicton** (53, 54) the formal Italian gardens and rectangular pond date from 1735, and must be one of the latest to be constructed in this style. All was swept away in the 18th century with the 'return to nature', when the formal layouts were drastically altered. Paths curved; streams meandered; bridges were rustic; trees were planted in picturesque copses and groves, and everyone had to have a 'wilderness'. Straight lines were consigned to the vegetable garden.

Devon seems not to have attracted any of the early landscape gardeners, such as Kent or Bridgeman. The great gardens were the work of their owners, influenced, no doubt, by visits to such estates as Stowe, and by their continental travels. This was still a remote county, reached only by several days of uncomfortable travel over rough roads. But when roads improved, and with increased wealth from agricultural rents and trade, many estate owners succumbed to the dictates of the newest fashions. 'Capability' Brown (1716–83) was lured to Devon, and in 1761 laid out **Ugbrooke Park** (51) for the Fourth Baron Clifford. Here he created 'a parkland free from artificial embellishments, a perfect composition of water, wood and grass.' Although the Robert Adam house was remodelled in 1874, the parkland escaped alteration, and remains a rare example of Brown's work in Devon. The parkland at **Saltram** (10) was the work of one of Brown's former assistants in conjunction with the owner, Lord Boringdon, and that, too, remains largely unaltered.

Humphry Repton (1752–1818), with his famous 'Red Books', was the next great name in the landscape world. There are only two known examples of his work in Devon: Luscombe Castle at Dawlish for the Hoare family, and **Endsleigh** (4), at Milton Abbot, for the Dukes of Bedford. Brown had favoured nature coming right up to the walls of the house, banning all forms of flowerbed and shrubbery, and to him is credited the invention of the ha-ha to keep grazing animals at a safe distance. Repton considered that a house and its occupants deserved something a little more sophisticated than grass, and terraces and flowerbeds returned to the scene.

The end of the 18th century saw a transformation in the gardening world, with new species flooding in from distant countries, sent home by plant-hunters. A new breed of nurserymen grew up, including the famous Veitch family of Exeter. John Veitch (1752–1839) came from Scotland, and before he reached the age of 20, had been commissioned to lay out the gardens at **Killerton** (42) for Sir Thomas Dyke Acland. Veitch went on to found his nursery nearby. This business and the firm of Luccombe financed and organized plant-hunting expeditions to

the Far East and the Americas. From the seed sent back, huge numbers of new plants were raised, and seedlings found their way to estates such as **Bicton** (53, 54), **Killerton** (42), **Arlington** (13), and **Endsleigh** (4). Many of the great arboreta date from this period, and some wonderful survivors from the original plantings can still be seen.

The 19th century

The 19th century was a time of great expansion and wealth. Wealth needed to be visible, so ostentation was the norm. Those who could afford it had terraces and fountains, elaborate greenhouses, and kitchen gardens producing exotic fruits and huge quantities of flowers to grace the house, not only in Devon but sent via the new railway system to the family's London residence during the Season. Flete (see 83) is the prime survivor from this era. Gardens became much more elaborate – labour was cheap and plentiful – and parterres and bedding schemes took over. Only municipal parks can afford this form of gardening now, as at the **Connaught Gardens** in Sidmouth.

in 1898). The work of Sir Edwin Lutyens can be seen in several places in the county – he designed **Castle Drogo** (91), but the garden is thought to be the work of George Dillestone, although the layout has all Lutyens' hallmarks. A little-known garden at Saunton Court in north Devon is by Lutyens (1932), with all his typical features, and both **Coleton Fishacre** (73) and Castle Tor in Torquay are the work of his pupils.

Devon is a landscape made up of small farms and manor houses with few grand mansions or great landowners. Those that do exist have been largely content to farm their Devon acres and not meddle in politics or follow fashionable pursuits, and this is largely true today. There are lost gardens aplenty here, but no-one has 'done a Heligan', or created a Woburn to become a major tourist attraction. Twentieth-century gardening has been very much scaled down, with only a few of the renowned designers being called in – Percy Cane at Flete and **Dartington** (75), and at the latter, Beatrix Farrand and Avray Tipping had a hand. The result of two World Wars is that gardens have become the preserve of their owners, with perhaps a few employees. Only tycoons can afford sufficient staff to maintain a grand garden, and it is noteworthy that Devon is attracting a few of these. But the county has an abundance of first-class gardeners, for whom their plot of ground is both their hobby and their relaxation. This body of men and women is both skilled and knowledgeable: people such as Lady Anne Palmer who created **Rosemoor** (32); the late Dr

The 20th and 21st centuries

The last great gardens on a grand scale date from the early 20th century, when Nesbitt and Mawson were working at Hannaford Manor, near Ashburton (1906), and Wood, near South Tawton (begun

Jimmy Smart at **Marwood** (29); the Heathcoat-Amory family who created **Knightshayes** (left; 43) and nearby Chevithorne, and the Fortescues at **The Garden House** (5) are the well-known examples; but there are many more who, collectively, have produced a tapestry of beautiful gardens varying in size from several acres to a 'postage stamp' around a cottage, all over the county. In Devon, you are never far from a good garden.

Public parks and gardens

Almost every town and village of any size in the county has a public open space of some description. The village green was the forerunner of the public park, where villagers congregated to pass the time of day, and where the fairs and village sports were held. Common land was plentiful, but with the Enclosure Acts of the late 18th century, and the subsequent migration of people from the land to the industrial centres, the need for open space for recreation became increasingly important. The Public Health Act of 1875 forced local authorities to make provision, but long before then most of Devon's towns and cities had public parks.

Exeter

The earliest public park still surviving is **Northernhay** in Exeter, which was laid out in 1612: records from this time show that there was a bowling green in the shelter of the city walls. It is possibly the earliest public garden in the country, on the site of the Roman excavations for the stone for the city walls, which today form one boundary with the railway line along the lower side. **Southernhay**, also in Exeter, is almost as old, and was originally a place where fairs were held outside the city walls. When this area was developed with elegant terraces and squares in the late 18th century, Southernhay became the central green. Today it is popular with office workers and visitors, who use it as a picnic area, enjoying the floral displays and shade from the many trees. A recent display commemorates the Veitch family and its long association with the city.

Exeter has many well-maintained parks and gardens throughout the city, which in summer seems to be a continuous floral display. Well worth a visit is the **University of Exeter** campus. This is centered around the former Streatham Hall, built in 1866 by a wealthy East India merchant who lavished £70,000 on laying out the grounds. The area is now home to the University buildings, but still contains the original Veitch arboretum, which has some magnificent trees and fine shrubs. Visitors can also enjoy the **Sculpture Walk** on the campus (which is larger than the grounds of the original Streatham Hall): the lovely natural landscape, enhanced by excellent planting, forms the perfect backdrop to the modern sculpture collection. This includes works by Hepworth, Moore, Ayrton, and Kawalec, among many others.

Plymouth

Plymouth lacks the intimate air of Exeter, and is a much busier and much larger city. Its earliest public space is **The Hoe**, made famous by Sir Francis Drake's game of bowls. Not until 1817 was it laid out formally, and it must be the only park to feature a lighthouse: Smeaton's origi-

nal Eddystone was rebuilt here in 1884 when it was replaced. There is also an imposing Naval War Memorial. The other great open space is **Central Park**, which was created out of farmland sold cheaply to the city by Lord St Levan, on condition that it remained public open space. The Ministry of Health gave approval for the use of unemployed labour, and the 234 acres (93.6ha) were laid out in 1929. The park contains the city's football stadium, and originally provision was made for cricket, tennis, swimming, golf, bowls – and parking for up to 700 cars. Sadly, the open space has been eroded for development, and more is threatened. Of historic interest is **Devonport Park**, close to the naval dockyard and on Ministry

of Defence land. The locals had taken to using the outer defences, and it was decided to regularize this by creating a park, which was finished by 1874, complete with fountains, flowerbeds, seats, and lodges. The **Civic Square** is an example of modern town planning, designed by Sir Geoffrey Jellicoe in 1959, between the new Civic Centre and the 19th-century Guildhall, as part of the restructuring of the city.

Torquay

Some of the earliest and most interesting public gardens originated as part of the development of seaside resorts. All along the coast, municipal flowerbeds and plantings enliven the seafront – the best in the larger resorts. Torquay was first developed from a fishing village in the late 18th century, when the naval fleet anchored in the bay and continental holidays were no longer possible – both the result of the Napoleonic wars. It was not until 1890 that the town acquired the seafront, and the harbour wall and promenade were built. Some 200,000 tons [203,200 tonnes] of spoil were used to reclaim land adjacent to the pier, and on this the **Princess Gardens** (left) were laid out.

The town's main beach, Abbey Sands, is named after the twelfth-century **Torre Abbey**. Once among the wealthiest English houses of the Premonstratensian canons, it was razed by Henry VIII. Today, the grounds are always open, and contain palm and cactus houses.

To the west of the town is **Cockington Court** (72), whose landscaped grounds are now maintained as public gardens.

Paignton

Paignton has its fair share of municipal gardens, but **Oldway Mansion** (right) is outstanding. Built by Isaac Singer (of sewing-machine fame), the design of the house is somewhat overpowering: it must be one the grandest council offices anywhere, with arguably the finest formal grounds still in existence in the county. Here, still maintained to a high standard, is the kind of garden that, in the Edwardian era, went with every house of any size.

Sidmouth

On the east Devon coast, Sidmouth attracted royal approval when the young Princess Victoria stayed in the recently developed resort. It is full of historic buildings, but it was not until 1934 that the superb **Connaught Gardens** were laid out on a site high above the sea, reached by a long (listed) flight of steps known as Jacob's Ladder. The gardens are on the site of Cliff Cottage, an 1820s villa purchased by the Council in order to create the public gardens, complete with an active band stand, restaurant, and dazzling floral displays.

Bideford, Barnstaple and Ilfracombe

On the North Devon coast, Bideford has a fine park on made-up ground, which is below the level of the adjacent River Torridge. It is well laid out, with playing fields, an art gallery, and a former bandstand. Barnstaple has a fine tradition of floral displays throughout the town, and Ilfracombe, developed in the mid-18th century, has a series of municipal gardens, but has lost its 'Crystal Palace' – a 60m (200ft)-long glass pavilion, which has been replaced by a theatre of futuristic design.

Much is owed to the commendable foresight of the local authorities of the day, who went to great lengths and considerable expense to provide public parks, open spaces, and gardens, and to protect their valuable sea frontages where otherwise huge areas would have been lost to development. It is to be regretted that today's authorities seem to favour selling off land for development rather than protecting it.

Times of opening

This Guide describes some 130 gardens in Devon open at the time of publication, the majority of which have been, and may be expected to remain open for many years. However, some of the smaller, private gardens, open for only a day or two annually, may change from year to year, when their owners, often retired or elderly, move or find opening too exacting, so it is always advisable to check in advance current times of opening. For this purpose, contact telephone, email and web details are given. Additional information about many of these gardens, and those for which contact numbers are not given, or that have opened since this book was published, may be found in the 'yellow book' – *Gardens of England*

How to Use this Book

and Wales Open for Charity, of the National Gardens Scheme (NGS), or on their website **www.ngs.org.uk**. Alternatively, you may send an A5 stamped, addressed envelope for a free 36-page booklet to: Devon NGS, Sutton Mead, Moretonhampstead, Devon TQ13 8PW. Several gardens may also open for other charities or local events, which may be advertised in the sources noted on page 238. Since hours of opening vary from year to year, opening times are given simply as 'am' (morning, usually from 10 a.m.) or 'pm' (afternoon, usually 2–5 p.m.), or 'am, pm' (morning and afternoon).

Please remember that most of the smaller gardens are private property, and are opened occasionally only through the generosity and enthusiasm of their owners. Do not assume that they can be entered at times other than those stated,

or that on the larger estates a charity opening implies any public rights of way. When approached with consideration, most gardeners will be happy to share their experiences with you.

Finding a garden

The gardens are grouped into six regions (each with a short introduction); arranged alphabetically within a region, and numbered sequentially throughout the Guide. For each entry, the name of the owner (who is not necessarily the person who will answer enquiries); the address; contact enquiry numbers, and road directions (given in miles [ml]) are provided.

Each garden has a grid reference, which applies equally to the Ordnance Survey *Landranger* 1:50 000 (one inch to the mile), and *Explorer* 1:25 000 (two and a half inches to the mile). In order to help you plan a garden visit, a 1:550 000 (approx. one inch to nine miles) map is provided inside the back cover of the Guide. Permanent brown road signs show the way to major gardens, and temporary yellow signs indicate gardens open under the NGS.

Appreciation and official ratings

Where appropriate, garden descriptions give information about the history of the site and the persons who created the garden, so that the plants and features may be appreciated in a wider perspective.

Some properties have been graded by English Heritage (**EH**). In such cases, the **gradings** for the house and garden are given separately. There are three grades – I, II*, or II. Similarly, landscape **designations** are given for the localities – **AONB**, the national designation for an *Area of Outstanding Natural Beauty* – and the two local designations – **SAGLV** for a *Special*

Area of Great Landscape Value, and **AGLV** for an *Area of Great Landscape Value*.

Size, aspect, soil and climate

For most gardens, the aspect, climate, soil and size are given. Temperatures are divided into zones, dependent upon the average minimum temperature in February, the coldest month in Devon. They are as follows:

A 5–4.5°C
B 4.5–4°C
C 4–3.5°C
D 3.5–3°C
E 3–2.5°C
F 2.5–2°C
G 2–1.5°C
H 1.5–0°C

Plants

Most gardens that open have their own plants for sale. These are distinguished from larger nurseries as follows: **plant centre** refers to a small 'nursery', such as those in some National Trust gardens; **nursery** signifies a commercial nursery associated with a garden, such as those at **Plant World** (86) and **Holbrook Garden** (40). There is a full list of other nurseries, not associated with gardens, on pages 247–8.

Some gardens listed have special plant collections registered by the National Council for the Conservation of Plants and Gardens (NCCPG). These **National Collections** (NC) are noted where they occur.

Facilities

Facilities differ from garden to garden. A key to the symbols used is given on the flap inside the front cover. If a symbol does not appear, the facility is not available – for example, wheelchair access – or

perhaps not allowed – for example, dogs. However, enquiries may be made in special cases. It is to be expected that guide dogs for the blind will always be admitted. A few National Trust gardens have a Braille guide and scented gardens.

Calendar

In order to find the gardens open at times convenient to you, the **Calendar** (pages 248–51) groups them in four sections:

1 Open throughout the year
2 Open on a regular basis
3 Open only on one or two days, arranged by months
4 Open by appointment only.

Each entry is cross-referenced to the more detailed entries in the Guide.

Note

The information in the Guide is accurate at the time of going to press. However, gardens may change their opening times, and neither the author nor the publishers are responsible for any such changes, which may occur without notice.

To the west of Dartmoor is Tamar country, the great river forming the boundary with Cornwall. Between its steep, tree-lined banks the Tamar flows down to Plymouth, past old quays and derelict buildings, the legacy of former industries – mining, fishing, and quarrying. Much of the wealth of the Dukes of Bedford came from their huge mining interests on the banks of the Tamar. The tourist development at Morwellham Quay gives a taste of the area's industrial past. In the 18th century a canal from Tavistock brought copper ore to this port. This part of Devon is isolated from the rest of the county, and has a distinctly Cornish feel, its villages rainwashed, and built of granite. Steep combes run down to the Tamar, and the few river crossings determine the pattern of settlements.

To the south, in the narrow belt of land between Dartmoor and the coast, is Plymouth, the largest city in Devon, yet separated from Cornwall only by the River Tamar. Its history has been dominated by the sea, and by the navy, to which the city is still home. Plymouth as such only came into being in 1914, when the three villages of Devonport, Sutton, and Stonehouse were formally amalgamated. The Barbican and the old harbour at Sutton are among the oldest surviving areas of a city that was devastated by German bombing in the Second World War. The famous navy base grew up at Devonport, centred around the great King William Victualling Yard, covering 14 acres (5.6 ha), but now sadly redundant. The breakwater, built in 1841, provided

1 WEST

anchorage for the fleet, and this area and the mouth of the Tamar are usually busy with maritime activity. Brunel's mighty Saltash bridge carries the railway west into Cornwall, and the newer road bridge has replaced the ferry that for centuries had been the only means of crossing. Much of the city had to be replanned and rebuilt after the Second World War, so it has a modern feeling, with wide streets and pedestrian areas built to a grid pattern.

open	Under NGS, 1 Jun–1 Sep, some Sat, Sun, am, pm, and by appt
directions	SX51 59, from A38 Forder valley junction follow signs for Estover, R into Novorissik Rd, L past ASDA, Keswick Cresc, 1st L
owners	Mr & Mrs D. Fenwick
address	96 Wasdale Gardens, Estover, Plymouth PL6 8TW
enquiries	T: 01752 301402 E: See website W: www. theafricangarden.com

WEST

SX51 59

P

size	Small
soil	Deep loam
rainfall	89–102cm/35–40in
temperature	Zone E
NC	*Tulbaghia, Crocosmia, Chasmanthe*
	Plant sales

Attracting a large number of visitors, and the subject of much media attention, this small garden is the work of David Fenwick, a specialist in southern African plants. A densely planted kaleidoscope of colour includes over 170 varieties of *Crocosmia*; about the same of *Kniphofia*; 120 varieties of *Amaryllis*, *Agapanthus*, and *Gladiolus*. In spring there are plenty of bulbs and David Fenwick, a former professional gardener, is now an acknowledged expert in his field. One of his aims is to promote the collection and conservation of bulbs from southern Africa, in order to carry out proper research and promote them to a wider public. Many of these plants have medicinal uses, and he feels that if they are grown widely enough in other countries, this will obviate the need for export from their native soil. His garden is a living example of how much can be achieved in a small space if the owner is dedicated and enthusiastic enough. Visitors are treated to an informative commentary, and David Fenwick also gives lectures to garden clubs, but prefers them to come to him rather than the other way round.

1 The African Garden

open	Mid-Feb–end Mar, pm; end Mar–end Oct, am, pm
directions	SX48 66, 11ml N Plymouth, 6ml S Tavistock, signed from A386 Plymouth–Tavistock. Car-park 150yd
owner	NT
address	Buckland Abbey, Yelverton PL20 6EY
enquiries	T: 01822 853607 E: bucklandabbey@nationaltrust.org.uk www.nationaltrust.org.uk
EH	House: I

WEST

SX48 66

size	1.2ha/3a
soil	Lime-free
altitude	600m/2,000ft
aspect	SW, AONB
rainfall	89–102cm/35–40in
temperature	Zone B

Once home to Sir Francis Drake, it was fitting that the National Trust should take sole charge of **Buckland Abbey** on the 400th anniversary of the Spanish Armada, in 1988. Drake's descendants had lived there until 1947, when it passed to the joint control of the Trust and Plymouth City Council. Major restructuring and renovation of the grounds have taken place since then, under the guidance of head gardener Sally Whitfield, who came to the Abbey in 1988. Her first task was to rescue the herb garden, instigated by Vita Sackville-West in the 1950s, when she was on the Trust's Garden Committee. This occupies a narrow space between the great barn and the abbey, dominated by its central tower. An intricate patchwork of 52 beds, edged in neatly-clipped box, are packed with a wide variety of herbs, many grown for their scent as well as their culinary and medicinal qualities. A recent addition is the Elizabethan garden laid out on the north side of the abbey, which replaces an ancient line of yews that had succumbed to root disease. Lavender and rosemary edge the beds around a central circular pool, and the beds are filled with plants in keeping with the abbey setting – old irises, columbines, peonies, and delphiniums. Old varieties of vegetables are grown in beds at the end of the garden. Beyond is the old orchard, where the grass is planted with wild tulips, narcissi, daisies and other wild flowers. Old plantings of rhododendrons and magnolias edge the lawns to the south, which contain a number of fine trees.

2 Buckland Abbey

open	Under NGS, one Sun each May, Jun, Sep, and by appt
directions	SX48 66, 8ml N Plymouth from A386 Plymouth–Tavistock follow signs Buckland Abbey, R at Xroad before Abbey, drive is 200 yd on L
owners	Mr & Mrs M. Stone
address	The Cider House, Buckland Abbey, Yelverton PL20 6EZ
enquiries	T: 01822 853285 E: michaelstone@ cider-house.co.uk
EH	House: II

WEST

SX48 66

P

size	1.2ha/3a
soil	Acid
altitude	90m/300ft
aspect	S + W, AONB
rainfall	114–127cm/40–45in
temperature	Zone E
	Plant sales

The old stone walls of this lovely cluster of buildings echo those of their grand neighbour, **Buckland Abbey** (2), of which they were once a part. The peace of monastic life still seems to pervade the fabric of The Cider House and its enchanting three-acre (1.2ha) gardens. The gardens lie to the rear of the house, and are entirely the creation of Michael and Sarah Stone. You could be forgiven for thinking that the granite paths, steps, little rills and ponds were as old as the buildings, but they were constructed out of a job lot of stone from the Devonport docks, when they were dismantled. The design was the subject of much discussion before the layout was finally decided, with help from a medieval historian.

The planting flows seamlessly from bulbs and camellias, through rhododendrons and azaleas in the far garden, to roses and herbaceous borders closer to the house. There is a herb garden and woodland. Each well-structured area is skilfully planted with contrasting plants, and the stream that runs through the garden is put to good use, channelled into ponds and a Lutyenesque rill that teems with tadpoles in spring. Vegetable-growing is becoming a lost art, but the productive walled garden, with neat rows of vegetables and lovely pillars of beans and sweet peas in summer, is an inspiration that counters this trend.

3 The Cider House

open	Please phone
directions	SX39 78, signed from B3362 Tavistock–Launceston
owner	Endsleigh Charitable Trust
address	Endsleigh, Milton Abbot, Tavistock PL19 0PQ
enquiries	T: 01822 870248
EH	House: I

WEST

SX39 78

EH	Gardens: I
size	26ha/65a
soil	Acid, free-draining
altitude	90m/300ft
aspect	W, AONB
rainfall	114–127cm/40–45in
temperature	Zone E

Until the sale of their Devon estates in 1962, Endsleigh was the holiday retreat and fishing lodge of the Dukes of Bedford – a welcome release from the grandeur of Woburn Abbey. The house itself was designed as a *cottage ornée* for the sixth Duke by Jeffrey Wyatt, in the early years of the 19th century. Following the sale, the estate was purchased by a fishing syndicate, which has managed it ever since. To the syndicate, gardens were less important than salmon, and although basic maintenance was carried out, it was not until 1989, when a Charitable Trust was set up, that the gardens were taken seriously. Since then, with the help of the Friends of Endsleigh, English Heritage, and various other funding bodies, the beautiful grounds have again been gaining the attention they deserve. The gardens, which are listed Grade I, contain 13 listed buildings and structures.

The Duke of Bedford created a garden on a grand scale: the long border is *very* long; there are cascades and an awe-inspiring rockery, as well as a Dairy (bottom right) and Swiss cottage – both now let as holiday homes by the Landmark Trust. Humphry Repton was called in, and prepared one of his famous Red Books; both he and Wyatt had a hand in the creation of the gardens, which perfectly complement the house. Recently, the head gardener has breathed fresh life into the borders and parterres, and the Dell Garden is beginning to be appreciated once more. Throughout the estate are wonderful, mature trees, many of them planted in the 1800s: the list of specimens makes impressive reading. There is an ongoing programme of restoration.

4 Endsleigh

WEST

SX49 68

size	3.20h/8a
soil	Light sandy
altitude	130m/420ft
aspect	W, AONB
rainfall	114–127cm/45–40in
temperature	Zone F
	Nursery

The nucleus of this well-known ten-acre (4ha) garden was created around the old walls and ruined tower of a medieval vicarage, by Lionel and Katharine Fortescue, over a period of 40 years after the Second World War. Fortescue is a name that crops up frequently in horticultural circles: Lionel was a connoisseur, and planted only the very best specimens in his garden. His policy was to prune plants hard; feed them well, and ruthlessly eradicate anything that did not do well. Shelter from the cold winds that sweep the north-facing slope was essential, and was provided by the now-towering *Cupressus leylandii* on the margins, with several internal partitions dividing the two-acre (0.8ha) walled garden. The whole garden is crammed full of interesting shrubs, trees, and perennials, with emphasis on camellias and rhododendrons.

After the Fortescues' deaths, The Fortescue Garden Trust was set up to preserve the gardens for future generations. In the years since 1978, garden manager Keith Wiley has greatly extended the garden, adding first the 'ovals garden' to the Walled Garden. From a small summerhouse, curving walls and paths descend to a circular paved area, originally planted with ribbons of blue *Corydalis* to give the effect of water tumbling down the slope. Keith Wiley's modern garden has interlinked themed areas inspired by the natural world, including a cottage garden, a fernery, a circle of monoliths, South African and Cretan gardens, an English meadow, and a spring bulb area – with views out over the Devon and Cornwall countryside. This is a garden for all seasons, with good ideas and good planting.

5 The Garden House

open	Under NGS, Mon–Fri, May–Sep, am, pm; by appt Sun, May–Sep
directions	SX46 86, from Lewdown on old A30 follow signs
owners	von Essen Hotels
address	Lewtrenchard Manor, Lewdown, Okehampton EX20 4PN
enquiries	T: 01566 783222 www.lewtrenchard. co.uk
EH	House: II

WEST

SX46 86

size	4.5h/11a
soil	Slightly acid loam
altitude	90m/300ft
aspect	Level, AGLV
rainfall	114–127cm/45–50in
temperature	Zone E

Sabine Baring Gould – one of the last of that interesting breed known as a 'Squarson', combining the duties of lord of the manor with those of parish priest – rebuilt the house in its present 'Jacobethan' form. He lived here from 1881 until his death in 1924 at the age of 89, and during his long life wrote many notable hymns and books, including novels, guidebooks and collections of West Country stories. The estate is now owned by the Baring Gould Corporation, and is part of the von Essen collection of country-house hotels.

The gardens, laid out by Baring Gould, have been brought back to life by the previous hoteliers, and are now in the capable hands of Robert Stemson, who has great plans for them, including the revival of the walled garden, and the reconstruction of an 80m-border designed by Gertrude Jekyll, the original plans of which have recently come to light. The sunken rose garden contains over 400 roses, and a 'holy well', from which a stream issues to feed the lily pond. Visitors can stroll along a circular walk, which takes in a bluebell walk under the beech avenue, the banks of the River Lew, and the woodland surrounding the former quarry, now a deep lake. Huge numbers of bedding plants are raised every year to fill the tubs, hanging baskets, and borders, so that the garden is colourful throughout the year.

6 Lewtrenchard Manor

open	Under NGS, one Sun each May, Jun, Jul, and by appt
directions	SX48 56, from Mutley Plain, R at Henders Corner into Eggbuckland Rd, 3rd R at tel kiosk to end of avenue
owners	Mr & Mrs M.H. Tregaskis
address	The Lodge, Hartley Avenue, Mannamead, Plymouth PL3 5HP
enquiries	T: 01752 220849

WEST

SX48 56

[P] [♟♟] [♿] [☕] [🐕]

size	Small
soil	Stony, neutral
altitude	90m/300ft
aspect	S
rainfall	89–102cm/35–40in
temperature	Zone D
	Plant sales

Could there be a garden worth the effort of visiting in Plymouth itself? It is sad that there aren't more, but tucked away in a remarkably secluded and quiet area is a surprising half-acre (0.2ha). From outside, the high walls and solid doors give little clue to what lies behind. Perched on a sunny ledge with views over what are now suburbs and allotments is The Lodge. Built *c.*1880, when the tall terrace behind was developed, it became the property of Plymouth City Corporation in the early 20th century, and was used as a nursery. When the present owners moved here in the 1970s, much of the garden was covered in concrete and derelict greenhouses, all of which had to be cleared away before they could begin the garden.

Sitting on the sun-drenched lawn, the city seems remote. Behind, a slope is closely planted with hardy ground-covers, such as geraniums, *Hypericum*, and heathers, all forming a colourful tapestry. The frothy little daisy, *Erigeron*, seeds itself everywhere. Along the perimeter wall at the top, a large greenhouse, which had to be rebuilt, houses tender climbers as well as a vast number of cuttings: almost everything that grows in the garden is propagated for sale. On this small site, good use is made of climbers, and the garden is divided by arbours, pergolas, and trellis-work – anything that can support a rose, clematis, golden hop, or some honeysuckle. At the far end is a large and very productive vegetable and fruit garden, with a couple of working beehives.

7 The Lodge

open	Under NGS, May–Sep, by appt
directions	SX47 83, from Lydford Gorge–Brentor road take road to Chillaton; R to Liddaton, downhill Liddaton X, sharp R; 400yd cross railway, immediately R; 0.5ml downhill L over small bridge
owners	Ms J. Hale & Mr A. Osborne
address	Longham, Coryton, Okehampton EX20 4AA
enquiries	T: 01822 860287

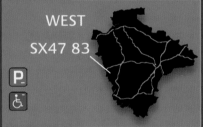

WEST

SX47 83

P.

(accessible)

size	0.3h/0.75a
soil	Neutral
altitude	60m/200ft
aspect	S, AGLV
rainfall	114–27cm/45–50in
temperature	Zone D

A cluster of redundant farm buildings and the cottage lying deep in the woods of the Lyd valley have provided an ideal base for Jennie Hale's pottery business. While she was busy setting up her kilns in 1982, Andrew Osborne was laying out the garden – a task made difficult by the bare concrete yard, and a collection of corrugated buildings, which had to be dug up and taken down. Initially Andrew planned a small nursery, and erected polythene tunnels for the stock, but now that his career as a garden designer has taken off, these are used for propagating his own plants.

The garden surrounding the cottage is full of lovely plants and good ideas. Pots and containers have been put to good use around the former yard areas, and the cottage has almost disappeared under creepers and climbers. The vegetable garden – an area developed early on – is both attractive and productive. The philosophy that if every patch of soil is planted to capacity, weeds won't stand a chance, seems to work well. The garden is very secluded, and one of its joys is the wildlife in the woods and along the riverbank. Deer browse in the fields, and on most days Jennie Hale disappears with her sketchbook to record the birds, fish, and insects from which she draws much of the inspiration for her work. Over the years this garden has become well known, and is well worth the navigational exercise required to reach it.

8 Longham

open	Under NGS, some Sun Jun, pm
directions	SX44 75, B3362 Tavistock–Launceston, L past Blacksmiths Arms to Chipshop, over Xroads Horsebridge, 1st L, L again
owners	Mr & Mrs I. Dingle
address	Portington, Lamerton, Tavistock PL19 8QY
enquiries	T: 01822 870364

WEST

SX44 75

size	1.2–8h/3–15a
soil	Loam. Peaty on shale
altitude	120m/400ft
aspect	S, AONB
rainfall	102–14cm/40–45in
temperature	Zone F
	Plant sales

In quiet countryside within a stone's throw of the Cornish border is Portington, a small cluster of cottages and farm buildings in an idyllic valley. The Dingles moved here from Plymouth in the 1970s: their relatives thought they were mad to bury themselves so far from civilization, and that they would soon be back. But never for one moment have they regretted it.

The garden did not take off properly until the children had grown up, but when it did it became an all-absorbing hobby. Lawns divided by borders, walks and pergolas occupy the level ground by the house, overlooking the meadow that slopes down to the stream and woodland. The planning is clever, although Maryan Dingle says that the garden 'just grew'. Ian Dingle says that his wife is the gardener, while he is just the 'doer'. His 'doing' includes the construction of slate walls, paths, paved areas, trelliswork and gates, bridges and the summerhouse. In 1988 he created a lake in the woodland, and at the top of the garden is his 'folly': what appears to be a ruined cottage is in reality just a wall with a door to the upper garden and the field behind.

Maryan Dingle has a keen eye for colour, favouring golden foliage contrasted with purple – a fine *Robinia* is grouped with a purple *Acer*. Narrow borders are interestingly planted, most with a trellis backbone so that clematis and roses give height, with shrubs and groundcover providing a bank of foliage and flowers. There is also a shady paved area and a scree slope. This garden is constantly evolving.

9 Portington

open	End Mar–end Oct, daily except Fri, am, pm
directions	SX51 55, 3ml E of Plymouth, follow NT signs
owner	NT
address	Saltram, Plympton, Plymouth PL7 1UH
enquiries	T: 01752 333500 E: saltram@nationaltrust.org.uk www.nationaltrust.org.uk
EH	House: I

WEST

SX51 55

EH	Gardens: II*
size	8h/20a
soil	Acid, sandy loam
altitude	45m/150ft
aspect	S + E
rainfall	89–102cm/35–40in
temperature	Zone D
	Plant sales

Built for the Parker family in the mid-18th century, Saltram is one of the West Country's most magnificent houses, containing a splendid set of state rooms designed by Robert Adam. It is surrounded by acres of parkland, which originally extended right up to the house. The present gardens were largely the work of the third Earl Morley, who planned them around the existing layout of rides in the 1880s. The property was acquired by the National Trust in 1957, and in 1963 a ha-ha was constructed to separate garden from grassland.

As befits a property of this nature, the gardens are on the grand scale. The Orangery, built in 1775 in classical style, was severely damaged by fire in 1932, but had to wait until 1961 for the Trust to restore it. The orange trees, grown in white Versailles tubs, are placed outside in spring, and return indoors in October. At the far end of the gardens is an octagonal summerhouse surrounded by mature woodland. Trees – many of them planted in the mid-19th century – are one of the glories of Saltram, and there is a fine 260m-long lime avenue, underplanted with narcissus and blue anemones. Over the years, *Cyclamen neapolitanum* has become naturalized in the garden, and produces clumps of delicate pink flowers from late summer onwards. There are banks of rhododendrons – some of them grown to huge proportions – camellias, and many magnolias. Herbaceous borders and banks of hydrangeas provide interest later in the year. This is a garden for all seasons.

10 Saltram House

open	Under NGS, one Sun each Jun, Jul; Jun–Aug, by appt
directions	SX51 56, from Marsh Mills roundabout follow signs Park & Ride, entrance just before
owners	Mr & Mrs M. Daly
address	Weighbridge Lodge, Longbridge Rd, Plymouth PL6 8LD
enquiries	T: 01752 261585

WEST

SX51 56

size	Small
soil	Neutral clay/sand
altitude	3m/10ft
aspect	Flat
rainfall	89–102cm/35–40in
	Plant centre

A small piece of history survives here, surrounded by urban sprawl. The Dalys' 19th-century cottage, built as part of the **Saltram** (10) estate, is enclosed by trees, with the river flowing past. In the 19th century, granite was brought by horse-drawn trucks along the rails that still pass the front of the cottage, across a small bridge and on to the docks at Plymouth. The cottage was derelict and vandalized when they bought it, and the garden was created partly on the bed of a former river – a difficult mix of clay and gravel – which had been used for years as an unofficial rubbish dump. The transformation is amazing: although the garden is small, on two sides of the cottage, and divided by outbuildings, an ingenious layout makes it seem larger. The different beds include some that are colour-themed, and some with special elements, such as a pond, a bog, and a newly planted dry garden of grasses, bamboos, *Euphorbia*, *Echinops*, and a tactile *Restio*. A huge beech tree, killed by lightning, is host to roses and clematis, and is underplanted with wild flowers and spring bulbs. *Phlox*, *Lysimachia*, and *Solidago* provide a long, colourful display, and demonstrate that these plants are long overdue for a return to favour.

11 Weighbridge Lodge

The rugged, Atlantic coast of north Devon faces the full fury of the westerly gales. Along this inhospitable coast there are few beaches, and only one safe harbour – that of Clovelly, protected by a jetty since the 14th century. The area is sparsely populated and very rural. Trees are stunted and leaning, and only the toughest of plants survive the salty blasts on the exposed headlands. Yet in sheltered valleys only a mile from the sea are two lovely gardens, at **Docton Mill** (19) and **Hartland Abbey** (24). Early in spring the hedgerows are awash with wild daffodils and primroses, and sea-pinks bring colour to the cliffs. Bideford Bay and Clovelly, on the Bristol Channel coast, are more sheltered, and the climate is milder. Much of the charm of the former fishing village of Clovelly is due to the abundance of flowers in hanging baskets and pots. The cobbled street runs down between cottages to the harbour, bordered on either side by small gardens where fuchsias and geraniums seem to bloom almost all the year round.

Bideford grew in size and prosperity in the 17th century, when trade with America expanded. The River Torridge had always been home to fishermen and seafaring folk, and the port was incorporated in 1573. At one time, Bideford was the second busiest port in the country, trading mainly in tobacco and fish with America and Newfoundland. Rich merchants built themselves large houses in and around the town, but modern development has encroached on most of them. **Tapeley Park** (35), on the opposite bank above Instow is a survivor, with its subtropical Italian gardens.

Bideford is still a port with a tree-lined riverbank, and **Victoria Park**, laid out in the early 1900s, is a fine example of municipal planting.

2 NORTH

The famous RHS garden at **Rosemoor** (32) is some nine miles inland in the sheltered valley of the Torridge, with its steeply wooded banks forming a fine backdrop below the hilltop market town of Great Torrington. This is farming country, where little has changed over the centuries – a patchwork of small fields and hedgerows, of woodland and isolated hamlets and farms, reached down winding lanes, where life has always been hard, and prosperity a stranger. To the south the land rises to the edge of Dartmoor, and the climate and scenery are bleaker.

open	Under NGS, last Sun in month, May–Aug, pm
directions	SS71 22, half-way between George Nympton and Alswear
owner	Mr R. Radford
address	Alswood House, George Nymtpon, South Molton EX36 4JH
enquiries	T: 01769 572321

NORTH

SX71 22

size	0.8–2.00h/2–4a
soil	Acid loam
altitude	135m/450ft
aspect	E
rainfall	89–102cm/40–45in
temperature	Zone F
	Plant sales

As a busy farmer, Bob Radford had little time for gardening; but when he retired in 1992, he wanted some form of outdoor occupation, so began to turn the former paddocks around the farm buildings into a garden. Having planted the area along the driveway with conifers, heather beds, and flowering shrubs, Bob Radford spread outwards. A bank was filled with rockery plants, a pond, and a cascade, and the barn behind draped with climbers. The latest project is a four-acre (1.6ha) arboretum on the highest ground, where about 120 trees are now becoming established. Bob Radford kept enough land to be able to spread himself: as one part of the garden fills up, he moves on to a new area, and digs a few more beds. Tall shrubs and trees divide the areas, and give structure to the overall design. Old farming implements provide focal points, and Bob Radford and his late wife created their own miniature Stonehenge out of redundant granite gateposts bought at a Dartmoor farm sale. There is great variety throughout this garden, with traditional herbaceous borders; newer grass and scree areas, and many varieties of clematis scrambling everywhere. Visitors can also enjoy lovely views of the Crooked Oak and Mole valleys from the garden.

open	Apr–Oct, daily except Sat, am, pm
directions	SS60 40, 7m NE Barnstaple on A39 to Lynton
owner	NT
address	Arlington Court, Barnstaple EX31 4LP
enquiries	T: 01271 850296 E: arlingtoncourt@ nationaltrust.org.uk www.nationaltrust. org.uk
EH	House: II*

NORTH

SS60 40

EH	Park: II*
size	12ha/30a
soil	Acid/neutral
altitude	120m/400ft
aspect	SW slope, AGLV
rainfall	89–102cm/35–40in
temperature	Zone C

The gardens at Arlington Court form a small part of the 30 acres (12ha) of pleasure grounds, which extend to include woodland, a lake, meadows, and the Wilderness. When the National Trust took over the property in 1949, it had been the home for almost 90 years of Miss Rosalie Chichester, the last of a long line of Chichesters connected with the estate. She was a keen naturalist, but had neglected the gardens: the formal Victorian gardens were completely overgrown, and the conservatory was derelict. It is only since 1993 that the borders and beds have been restored and a new, smaller conservatory erected.

Standing guard over the entrance steps are two herons with wriggling eels in their beaks – the crest of the Chichesters, which is to be found throughout the estate. This area is not large, but has a pond, herbaceous borders, Victorian basket beds, and honeysuckle trained over a row of arches. Volunteers were called in to clear the walled kitchen garden – a task that included uncovering the paths and clearing away the collapsed greenhouses. A range of fruit trees, mainly Devon varieties, and vegetables is now grown here. In spring, bluebells carpet the woodland and huge banks of rhododendrons make a beautiful display. Throughout the estate are numerous fine trees, many of them planted in the mid-19th century, when the lake, now popular with birdwatchers, was formed by damming the River Yeo.

13 Arlington Court

open	One Sun Jun, am, pm, and by appt from May
directions	SS55 36, B3230 Barnstaple–Ilfracombe, signed
owners	Mr & Mrs L. Shapland
address	Barleycott, Blakewell, Barnstaple EX31 4ES
enquiries	T: 01271 375002

NORTH

SS55 36

size	1.5ha/3.66a
soil	Thin, acid
altitude	60m/200ft
aspect	S, sloping
rainfall	89–100cm/35–40in
temperature	Zone F

In 1989 the Shaplands had a vision: standing at the highest point of their grass fields, they planned a lime avenue. Then a lavender walk, then a long path. The plans became a reality, and the gardens had begun. Since then they haven't stopped, and every year brings some new project – the tiny Japanese garden tucked away at the far end being one of the most recent. Paths and borders are constantly being altered, either for ease of maintenance – for the Shaplands are the only workers – or to incorporate new ideas. Until 2000, their home was the Old Mill, but when the chance arose to buy the barn and field next door, they jumped at it. A 'hanging garden' with a waterfall and pond occupies the lowest level by the newly converted barn, and a series of terraces takes the visitor to the top of the garden. Many of the herbaceous plants are raised by Babs Shapland, and most of the shrubs and trees, including many unusual varieties, are bought from local specialist nurseries; some were grown from seed – the gift of Roy Lancaster. This is a fine garden to wander around slowly, resting on one of the many seats, and enjoying the views and different aspects.

14 Barleycott

open	Early Apr–early Jun, Mon, Fri, am, pm; groups by appt all year
directions	SS67 28, between Barnstaple and South Molton, off N Devon link road
owners	The Earl & Countess of Arran
address	Castle Hill, Filleigh, Barnstaple EX32 0RH
enquiries	T: 01598 760336, Ext 4 www.castlehilldevon.co.uk
EH	House II*

NORTH

SS67 28

EH	Landscape: I
size	20ha/50a
soil	Acid, thin
altitude	120m/44ft
aspect	S + W, AGLV
rainfall	76–89cm/30–35in
temperature	Zone D

The long, yellow façade of Castle Hill, home to the Fortescue family since 1719, has long been familiar to travellers on the former main road to Barnstaple. This road cuts across one of the most important of historic landscapes in Devon, and there was a threat that the new link road would have come even closer to the house. Fortunately, this was built on the other side of the hill, and the landscape remains undisturbed.

The original park was laid out in the first half of the 18th century, and included a cruciform lake; terraces; the castle on the hill behind the house; the triumphal arch, and long avenues of trees. The grounds were radically altered and simplified in the 19th century, when natural landscapes were in fashion, but many of the original trees and garden buildings survive. The woodlands – a carpet of flowers in the spring – are planted with magnolias, camellias, rhododendrons, azaleas, and other flowering shrubs. The Fortescue family has continued to plant fine trees, and to maintain and restore the temples, seats, and other 18th-century buildings. Lady Arran, descendant of the Fortescue family, maintaining the tradition that every generation should add to the house and grounds, has created a Millennium garden between the house and the entrance drive: the highly acclaimed design is the work of Xa Tollemache. With its long border of lavender, lollipop trees of holm oak, and mixed herbaceous planting, the new garden is a fitting addition to Castle Hill. The latest addition to the design is a specially commissioned 'topiary' water sculpture by Giles Rayner, made of copper piping to echo the shape of the cupola on the house, over which water trickles.

open	Under NGS, one Sun Jun, Jul, pm
directions	SS59 12, from A3124 Torrington–Exeter road turn S (R) Stafford Moor Fisheries, 1st R
owners	Mr & Mrs T. Hynes
address	Higher Cherubeer, Dolton EX19 8PP
enquiries	T: 01805 804265
EH	Cherubeer: II

NORTH

SS59 12 ——

size	Small
soil	Acid clay
altitude	150m/500ft
aspect	S
rainfall	76–89cm/30–35in
temperature	Zone D
	Plant sales

The gardens of this tiny hamlet, consisting of a farm and two cottages, have lovely views over the fields to the village of Dolton; the church tower prominent in the near distance, with the wooded valley of the River Torridge beyond, and Dartmoor on the horizon. The winds cutting across the valley can be a problem, and for this reason the gardens of **Higher Cherubeer** are protected by belts of trees and high hedges. Jo and Tom Hynes were the first of the family to move here, in 1990, with no intention of farming; however, letting the land proved unsatisfactory, so Jo Hynes found herself getting involved with cattle and sheep. Her garden is home to rare breeds, fowls and ducks. The neighbouring cottages later became home to both sets of parents, and between them the gardens represent different styles and fashions in gardening. **Middle Cherubeer** makes full use of the views, and is a small, well-planted garden with lilac, pinks, saxifrage, and thyme – all the plants of our grandmothers' gardens, now often displaced by more fashionable imports. Jo Hynes' mother has a secret garden adjoining her lovely thatched cottage, with cobbled paths, a small pond, and plenty of pots all around the house. At **Higher Cherubeer** – the largest of the gardens – willow is a prominent feature, as Jo Hynes grows it to make baskets, hurdles, and screens. Sunflowers are grown for bird food, and everything is organic. Around the house, the former farmyard is now a more formal area with terraced beds, a scree area, and an alpine amphitheatre. The dry-stone walls were built by Tom Hynes, who mastered the skill when they lived in Lancashire.

16 Cherubeer Gardens

open	Apr–Sep, am, pm
directions	SS47 46, from Lee village down to seafront; park in car-park. 250yd up road, through wrought-iron gates on L
owner	Mrs Veronica Gilbert
address	Cliffe, Lee, Ilfracombe EX34 8LR
enquiries	T: 01271 862479

NORTH

SS47 46

size	2ha/5a
soil	Neutral silt
altitude	20–70m/66–230ft
aspect	NE
rainfall	100cm/39in
temperature	Zone D
NC	*Schizostylis* and *Heuchera*

Overlooking the village of Lee, and with views across the Bristol Channel to the Welsh coast, few gardens are closer to the sea than Cliffe. The property has been in the same family for three generations, with the gardens first laid out in the 1920s by Charles Pilley. He created the terraces and distinctive slate walling found throughout the garden. His daughter-in-law, Mrs Irene Pilley, took over – a keen and knowledgeable gardener, who at one time employed eight men in a garden that was at that time maintenance-intensive. Half of the five acres (2ha) are under cultivation; the rest is woodland, planted with rhododendrons, camellias and spring bulbs. Many of the plantings date from Mrs Pilley's time, and include a *Parrotia persica*, cordylines and phormiums, magnolias, azaleas and roses. Mrs Gilbert, her niece, grassed over the formal rosebeds, and simplified much of the planting. The site is not easy: rain- and windswept, with silty soil, a high level of sunshine in summer, but none throughout the winter months, so that spring comes late here. The main border as you enter the garden through the wrought-iron gates is closely planted with Mediterranean subjects – *Agaves*, *Agapanthus*, *Cistus*, *Hebes* and *Helianthemum*. The garden has National Collections of *Schizostylis* and *Heuchera*.

This is an entrancing garden, in a beautiful position, with magnificent views from every level. However, the steep nature of the site, its many steps and winding paths make it unsuitable for the infirm or less active visitor.

NORTH
SS56 23

P

size	0.4ha/1a
soil	Clay/acid
altitude	130m/450ft
aspect	SW
rainfall	89–100cm/35–40in
temperature	Zone E
	Plant sales

Despite having lived in this attractive north Devon village since 1976, it is only recently, since she retired, that Mrs Jewell has been able to devote herself to gardening. The Croft occupies a beautiful position, with wide views over the surrounding tranquil rural landscape, and a great variety of plants and garden styles have been skilfully incorporated. An artificial stream feeds a pond; a rose garden commemorates Mrs Jewell's mother, who also loved gardening; there is a long herbaceous border; and the former cottage garden is gradually being changed into an area devoted to plants grown for their foliage. The newest interest is Japanese gardening, and Mrs Jewell has built a replica Japanese tea-house overlooking the pond and cascade. The Croft demonstrates how a garden evolves over the years as the owners' interests change. An intricate system of paths leads the visitor to each area in turn – over bridges; up steps; around corners, and back to the central lawn. There is an abundance of garden ornaments, all painted black. The oldest plant is a eucalyptus, bought from Woolworth's when the Jewells first moved in, which has grown into a towering tree, and forms the backdrop to the Japanese garden.

18 The Croft

open	1 Mar–31 Oct, daily, am, pm
directions	SS23 22, follow brown tourist signs from A39 Bideford–Bude road
owners	Mr & Mrs J. Borrett
address	Docton Mill, Lymebridge, Hartland EX39 6EA
enquiries	T: 01237 441369 www.doctonmill.co.uk
EH	Millhouse: II

NORTH

SS23 22

size	3.6ha/9a
soil	Heavy clay
altitude	60m/22ft
aspect	N slope, level, AONB
rainfall	76–89cm/30–35in
temperature	Zone D
	Plant sales

Less than a mile from the rugged north Devon coast with its fierce westerly gales, is the garden of Docton Mill, sheltering in a wooded valley. The sound of water is everywhere, for the garden was created around the tumbling stream that runs past the former mill (complete with working water-wheel), and the mill leat that bisects the garden. Docton Mill has been fortunate in having a succession of keen gardening owners. In 1938, Miss Bianca Duncan planted native trees on the slopes above her home, and an apple orchard, with many now rare varieties. She planned the cobbled paths and flights of shallow steps that form the courtyard garden by the house. This sunny, sheltered area was planted with small plants and rockery subjects in terraces. A period of neglect ended in 1980 when Steve and Iris Pugh moved in. For 15 years they cleared, planted and renovated the garden, and restored the mill mechanism. The trees are now mature, and under the canopy are camellias, rhododendrons, and hydrangeas. Flowering cherries overhang the water, and in spring daffodils and primroses are everywhere. The Pughs planted banks of musk roses, and extended the garden down the valley. A collection of magnolias, planted in 1999, forms a living memorial to Iris Pugh. By now the garden was becoming well known: the next owners had to provide a car-park, and opened a tea room. The present owners, John and Lana Borrett, took over in 2000, maintaining the expert gardening tradition of the previous owners.

19 Docton Mill & Garden

open	Under NGS, early Apr–early Jul, daily, am, pm
directions	SS47 21, on A386 Bideford–Torrington road, between Landcross and Torrington
owners	Mr & Mrs R.C. Stanley-Baker
address	The Downes, Monkleigh EX39 5LB
enquiries	T: 01805 622244

NORTH

SS47 21

size	2ha/4.4a
soil	Clayish
altitude	90m/300ft
aspect	E slope, AGLV
rainfall	76–89cm/30–35in
temperature	Zone E
	Plant sales

Situated on a hilltop overlooking the valley of the River Torridge, The Downes has been in the same family for nearly 100 years. It was Helen Stanley-Baker's childhood home, and when she and her husband returned from colonial service in 1973, they carried on where her parents had left off. Although by then the garden was very overgrown in some areas, the legacy of mature trees and rhododendrons enabled them to develop a fine garden on this outstanding 15-acre (6ha) site. Some of the original pines and conifers have succumbed to the gales, but Charles Stanley-Baker is a keen arborist, and has added many interesting species throughout the garden, with a former tennis-court now a flourishing arboretum. The woods contain magnolias and azaleas, and in spring are thickly carpeted with bluebells. Nearer the house are banks of rhododendrons, hydrangeas, and herbaceous borders. A series of sheltered areas has been planted with smaller, more tender plants and some interesting rockery specimens. A prized specimen is the old *Acer palmatum dissectum* with its network of beautiful, twisted branches. The house walls are covered with glorious climbing roses, clematis, and several tender species, including a *Paulownia imperalis* and *Abutilon megapotomicun*. Spring is especially lovely, with camellias and daffodils lining the drive. Clematis feature throughout the garden, growing over old stumps and hedgerows, and into some of the trees. Everywhere there are fine views over the valley, and there is a woodland trail for children to enjoy.

20 The Downes

open	Under NGS, May, Jun, Aug, one Sun each, and by appt
directions	SS72 45, off A39 Barnstaple–Lynton road, turn R past Total Garage at Barbrook, 2m up lane on L
owners	Mr & Mrs D. Sydenham
address	Durcombe Water, Furzehill, Barbook, Lynton EX35 6LN
enquiries	T: 01598 753658

NORTH

SS72 45

size	0.6ha/1.5a
soil	Stoney, poor, slightly acid
altitude	275m/900ft
aspect	SW, Exmoor Nat Park
rainfall	127–140cm/50–55in
temperature	Zone G

An unfrequented lane climbs steeply from Barbrook, and for three miles runs along the ridge towards the rolling heights of Exmoor. Almost at its end is a cluster of cottages. The Chains dominates the landscape, benign and heather-clad in summer; threatening and rain-soaked in winter. But the garden at Durcombe Water is in a sheltered dip, surrounded by protective trees, with a stream at its heart. The garden was completely reworked in 1990, with the creation of cascades, ponds, and terraces, and the planting of many shrubs and trees, including conifers. The present owners moved here in 2001, and have developed this framework. Many of the shrubs had outgrown their space and had to go, but the trees form a major element, giving shape, and autumn colour. New areas have recently been created from the former paddocks and fields at the very top of the garden, and here the influence of the moor is felt. More trees have been planted, along with rhododendrons and bluebells; below is a timber pergola, separating the new garden from the old; a large fruit-cage and vegetable garden, and the greenhouse. Here David Sydenham propagates thousands of herbaceous plants and annuals every year, and after the spring display of bulbs, primulas, heathers, and azaleas, they take over, filling the beds and borders with colour for many months.

Once every summer, two neighbouring gardens join with Durcombe Water in opening for a local charity.

open	Mar–Sep, Wed, Thu, Fri, some Sun, am, pm, and by appt
directions	SS65 22, B3226 South Molton–Crediton road, R at Clapworthy Mill X towards Warkleigh; R at Fire Beacon X; L Swing Gate X, lst L
owner	Mrs C. Klein
address	Glebe Cottage, Pixie Lane, Warkleigh EX37 9DH
enquiries	T: 01769 540554

NORTH

SS65 22

size	0.4ha/1a
soil	Very heavy clay
altitude	170m/540ft
aspect	S, AGLV
rainfall	76–89cm/170m
temperature	Zone D
	Nursery

In 1990, Carol Klein was given just four weeks' notice to prepare a display for the RHS Chelsea Flower Show. She worked around the clock, and was rewarded with a silver medal. Since then, she has won six gold medals, and numerous other awards. She has presented television programmes; written garden articles, and lectured widely.

In the garden at Glebe Cottage, 'We only grow plants we consider garden-worthy, easy to cultivate, and with a long season of interest. We love our plants, and when you take them home we want them to flourish for you,' she says. This sums up Carol Klein's philosophy. Among the garden beds are large numbers of containers, some with stock plants for exhibits; some waiting to have their contents planted out; others just seem to belong here. The one-acre (0.4ha) garden is set in a remote part of rural north Devon, and is reached by a track across a field. To many, it is a place of pilgrimage – to learn as well as to buy. Here you will find many ideas relevant to small gardens. Carol Klein's garden rises in terraces to Glebe Cottage, with a wide range of situations, from a small woodland and stumpery, to a hot, arid bed at the top of the garden. Carol Klein has bred several named varieties of her favourite species, and produces an informative catalogue.

22 Glebe Cottage

open	Under NGS, one Sun each, Apr–Jul, Sep, Oct, pm, and groups by appt
directions	SS57 33, 1ml E Barnstaple on Bratton Fleming road, entrance between 2 lodges on L
owners	Dr J.A. Marston
address	Gorwell House, Goodleigh Road, Barnstaple EX32 7JP
enquiries	T: 01271 323202
EH	House: II

NORTH

SS57 33

size	1.6ha/4a
soil	Lime-free
altitude	60m/200ft
aspect	SW
rainfall	89–102cm/35–40in
temperature	Zone F
	Plant sales

Gorwell House was built in 1825, when Barnstaple was a distant town on the River Taw. Since then, the town has spread, and newer houses all but obscure the views over the estuary to Lundy. A new, four-acre (1.6ha) garden planted on ground above the house by Dr Marston, who has lived here since 1976, contains many rare trees and shrubs, which are growing into fine specimens. The large plateau is divided into areas by means of hedges and closely planted borders: there are avenues and long vistas, as well as small, intimate corners. This area was once a field grazed by bullocks, and Dr Marston originally had ideas for parkland dotted with a few trees. He planted the first – a tulip tree – in 1977; evicted the bullocks in 1982, and has been planting ever since. At intervals throughout the garden there are summerhouses; temples; a shell house; garden seats, and statuary. Closer to the house, Dr Marston's wife, Vanessa, displays her own sculpture. She works to commission and exhibits at the RHS Chelsea Flower Show. Above the house is a sheltered garden with a pergola, roses, and herbaceous borders. The house used to be sheltered from the prevailing winds by mighty elms, but in 1979, 40 of them had to be felled, due to Dutch elm disease. New shelter-belts have replaced these trees, allowing the more tender plants to thrive.

23 Gorwell House

open	House + gardens: Wed, Thu, Sun, bank holidays; + Tue, Jul, Aug, pm Gardens only: Apr–early Oct, daily except Sat, pm
directions	SS25 35, between Bideford and Bude, off A39, tourist signs to Hartland Quay
owners	Sir Hugh & Lady Stucley
address	Hartland Abbey, Hartland EX39 6DT
enquiries	T: 01237 441264/234
EH	House: I

NORTH

SS25 35

size	12h/30a approx
soil	Light, slightly acid
altitude	60m/200ft
aspect	W, AONB
rainfall	76–89cm/30–35in
temperature	Zone C

In this remote north-western corner of Devon is one of the oldest buildings in the county – a 12th-century abbey built by Augustinian monks. Since the dissolution of the monasteries, when Henry VIII gave the property to the keeper of his wine-cellar, Hartland Abbey has been occupied continuously by his descendants. The monks had fish-ponds, which are still visible, and walled gardens, and later on the whole valley became a deer park. The formal gardens that surrounded the Abbey disappeared long ago, when the monastery was dissolved, and were replaced with parkland and several fine trees. Much of the stonework, including two of the bridges across the river, dates from the monastic period.

Hartland Abbey owes much to its beautiful setting. In spring the woodlands abound in snowdrops, daffodils, primroses, and bluebells, with banks of rhododendrons and azaleas closer to the house. The garden also has an impressive collection of hydrangeas. Both the present Lady Stucley and her late mother-in-law have worked hard to restore and revitalize the gardens. The newly restored 18th-century walled garden, hidden away at the beginning of the drive, is their work. Wavy topiary hedges, an ancient mulberry, shrub roses, herbs, and sub-tropical plants thrive in the sunny shelter of the walls. Gertrude Jekyll was consulted on the planting both here and in the bog garden on the hillside – the latter was planted with camellias by Sir Hugh's father. In 1998 a Victorian fernery was discovered, and has now been replanted. Peacocks roam the grounds, and donkeys and black Welsh mountain sheep graze in the meadows. This is a magical place.

24 Hartland Abbey

open	Under NGS, one Sun end Jun, and by appt
directions	SS67 45, Barnstaple–Lynton road A39, 400 yd up hill from village centre, drive on R
owner	Mrs J. Keatley
address	Heddon Hall, Parracombe EX39 4QL
enquiries	T: 01598 763409
EH	House: II

NORTH

SX08 63

size	2ha/5a
soil	Neutral–acid, thin
altitude	240m/800ft
aspect	S, Exmoor Nat Park
rainfall	170–183cm/65–70in
temperature	Zone E
	Plant centre

Gardening is on a grand scale at Heddon Hall. Since 1990, a knowledgeable and experienced gardener has created five acres (2ha) of horticultural delights. The long drive down to the 19th-century former rectory gives little hint of what is in store as it passes between the young trees and shrubs of the new arboretum. Around the house are a formal terrace with a good collection of climbers; long borders planted with roses, and lawns that slope down to a pond. Passing through a quiet courtyard, which, in late spring is covered in white valerian, an explosion of colour from a hot bed crowded with sun-loving plants, greets the visitor. This bed is backed by an old stone wall, on the other side of which is the jewel in the crown – a beautiful walled garden, designed by Penelope Hobhouse. Clipped box hedges emphasize beds planted with a profusion of old English roses, cottage and herbaceous plants, herbs and vegetables; violas carpet the shady areas, and in summer, sweet peas are trained up poles. Some of the roses, pears, and peaches on the walls are very old, and remain from earlier plantings. Flourishing in the warmth of the walls are unusual, tender shrubs, many brought back from Jane Keatley's plant-hunting expeditions. Against the shady wall is a collection of ferns, and on the outer side a little arbour, and a frame of pleached limes. The River Heddon tumbles off Exmoor, beneath tree-covered banks planted with ferns, primulas and bog plants, before emerging into the sunlit lower garden, where it feeds the pond.

There are many horticultural rarities at Heddon Hall, and many plants from overseas, all specially chosen, and carefully labelled. Several famous gardeners, including Roy Lancaster and Carol Klein, have given help and advice.

25 Heddon Hall

open	By appt
directions	SS66 21, 4ml SW South Molton on B3226
owners	Mr S. Abell
address	Higher Watertown, Umberleigh EX37 9HF
enquiries	T: 01769 540470
EH	House: II

NORTH

SS66 21

size	0.2ha/0.5a
soil	Loam/clay neutral
altitude	75m/250ft
aspect	W, level, AGLV
rainfall	89–102cm/35–40in
temperature	Zone D
	Wholesale nursery

A homestead on this site is recorded in the 'Domesday Book', although the present house dates from the 16th century, and has a range of outbuildings left over from its days as a farm. The owners moved to the lush valley setting of the River Mole over 30 years ago, and ran the property as a smallholding. It was only in 2001 that they retired and handed over the garden and outbuildings to their son, Steve Abell. He had trained in horticulture, and spent over a decade in Cheshire working as a wholesale nurseryman. Back in his childhood home, he set up his business in the outbuildings and farmyards, raising plants in bulk for the wholesale trade. The nursery specializes in grasses and herbaceous perennials, and some lovely *Crocosmia* hybrids are available. The garden is being transformed. Already many of the lawns have disappeared, but Steve Abell has the advantage of working within a mature framework, much of it planted when he was a small boy. There is a trellis he remembers erecting when he was 16 years old, and a beautiful *Amelanchier* he has watched grow from a small seedling. The borders are now planned to have a backbone of colour throughout the year, with many of Steve Abell's stock plants flowering on either side. Many of the taller shrubs and trees started life in pots, which Steve Abell finds useful, as he can move them around the garden to find just the right place, and to fill bare gaps. Acers in particular seem to lend themselves to this treatment.

26 Higher Watertown

open	Under NGS, last Sun Jun, Jul, Aug, and groups by appt
directions	SS64 29, 1ml E of Swimbridge on Barnstaple–South Molton road, R at top of hill, immediately fork L
owners	Mr & Mrs P. Duncan
address	Kerscott House, Swimbridge, Barnstaple EX32 0QA
enquiries	T: 01271 830943 E: jessica@ kerscottgarden.co.uk www.kerscottgarden. co.uk

NORTH

SS64 29

size	2.4h/6a
soil	Shillet to clay
altitude	120m/400ft
aspect	Undulating, AGLV
rainfall	76–89cm/30–35in
temperature	Zone F
	Plant sales

Six acres (2.4ha) of windswept, stodgy, poorly drained clay have been transformed into a fine garden by the owner, Jessica Duncan, in the years since 1984. She believes that gardening should be fun, and her visitors, including children, enjoy the results. In the middle of a grove of silver birch there is a turf labyrinth. Dotted around the garden are animals made from chicken wire, stone, or topiary: look out for the fighting hares, which seemed to come naturally from two branches of the *Lonicera nitida* 'Baggesen's Gold' that forms a circle around the sunken garden in front of the house. Willow has been trained to create small arbours and windbreaks here, long before it became fashionable. Several ponds have been excavated, and the Duncans have planted hundred of trees, initially to form a shelterbelt, but latterly as an arboretum. It is important to them that the garden should harmonize with the surrounding countryside, and to this end they plant native trees and shrubs at the boundaries of the garden. Each new area becomes part of the whole design, with carefully planned views and vistas at every turn. Redundant farm buildings have been included: when the roof blew off a barn, the remaining shell was turned into a courtyard garden, a home for tender climbers. Visitors will want to keep returning to this garden to admire each new, inventive development.

27 Kerscott House

open	Under NGS, one Sat, Sun Jul, and by appt
directions	SS49 26, 2.5 ml E Bideford on Alverdiscott road
owners	Mr & Mrs J. Yewdall
address	Little Webbery, Alverdiscott Bideford EX39 4PS
enquiries	T: 01271 858206
EH	House: II

NORTH

SS49 26

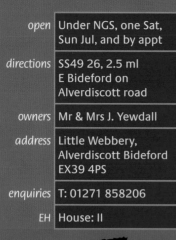

P

size	1.5h/3.5a
soil	Stony/neutral
altitude	90m/300ft
aspect	NW
rainfall	76–89cm/30–35in
temperature	Zone E
	Plant sales

Created in the early 1900s, the gardens of **Little Webbery** have now reached a beautiful state of maturity. Of traditional design, and set in quiet north Devon countryside against a backdrop of trees, they surround a small, 19th-century manor house. The wide herbaceous borders have deep blue delphiniums; lupins, poppies, peonies, and all the smaller favourites to be found in country-house gardens. Smooth, green lawns sweep down to the pond and merge into the fields, separated from the garden by two ha-has. Roses and lavender grow around the house, and everything is beautifully cared for by the full-time gardener who, together with the owners, has introduced many new features in the last 20 years. In spring there are banks of camellias and azaleas, with drifts of daffodils; but it is the roses that are the main feature, and the surprise comes on opening the door to the walled garden.

There are roses everywhere: over the walls, over arches, along poles and in neat, lavender-edged beds. Vegetables and soft fruits are also grown in the neat, box-edged beds. A nice touch throughout the garden is the names of plants painted on flat pebbles.

The garden of **Little Webbery Cottage**, occasionally open, is a charming small area, similarly planted, with roses and clematis climbing up and through many of the shrubs and trees.

28 Little Webbery &
Little Webbery Cottage

open	Daily except 25 Dec, am, pm
directions	SS54 37, 4ml N Barnstaple, tourist signs from A361 to Braunton and B3230 Ilfracombe road
owner	Dr J.A. Snowdon
address	Marwood Hill, Marwood, Barnstaple EX31 4EB
enquiries	T: 01271 342528 www.marwoodhill garden.co.uk

NORTH

SS54 37

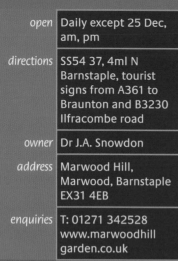

size	7.3h/18a
soil	Neutral/acid
altitude	100m/350ft
aspect	N and S
rainfall	89–102cm/35–40in
temperature	Zone E
NC	*Astilbe, Iris ensata, Tulbaghia*
	Nursery

The death of Dr Jimmy Smart in 2002 left a large gap in Devon's horticultural world, for Dr Smart was an acknowledged expert, and his legacy at Marwood Hill is exceptional. Together with his long-time head gardener, Malcolm Pharoah, who continues here, he planned and planted a garden that spreads out from the house, down to the valley where they created two lakes, and up on to the far hillside, covering some 18 acres (7.3ha). Initially, camellias were Dr Smart's great interest. Many new varieties were raised here and some of the original plantings, dating from the early 1960s, survive. Two large greenhouses are devoted to the species, and another to tender Australasian plants.

Although Dr Smart was essentially a plantsman, and everything is carefully labelled, he blended his schemes together, discarding second-rate plants, and leaving well alone those that were thriving. Some of the early trees are now enormous: flowering cherries with long branches bending down to the water; groves of eucalyptus, pines, and huge rhododendrons. What began as a hobby rapidly became an obsession. Many of the plants raised at Marwood gained RHS Awards of Merit, and Dr Smart's horticultural knowledge was in great demand.

This is one of Devon's finest gardens, which continues to delight over 16,000 visitors each year.

29 Marwood Hill

open	Bank hol early, late May, Aug + one Sun Jun, Jul, am, pm, and by appt
directions	SX53 99, follow A386 north from A30 at Sourton Services. After 3ml, turn L towards Northlew at Hilltown X, 3ml at bottom of steep hill, R towards Inwardleigh. 2nd entrance on L
owners	Mr & Mrs J. Barton
address	Milland Farm, Inwardleigh, Okehampton EX20 3BX
enquiries	T: 01837 810313 E: milland.farm@ btopenworld.com.

NORTH
SX53 99

P

size	0.4h/1a
soil	Clay
altitude	120m/130ft
aspect	W + S
rainfall	102–114cm/40–45in
temperature	Zone F
	Plant sales

When Julia and John Barton moved to this peaceful, sheltered corner of Devon in the early 1990s, they set about designing the garden from scratch. Julia is an artist, and as so often happens with artist-gardeners, the colours and shapes blend especially well in the design of this garden. The first area to be planted was a circular herb garden, which is quartered with beds devoted to aromatic, culinary, medicinal, and dye-yielding herbs. The centrepiece is a fountain, with water coming up through an old tree stump rescued from the nearby riverbank. The land rises gently to a pretty summerhouse looking out over the 13 acres (5.25ha) of fields to the woods of the river valley. The Bartons encourage all forms of wildlife here, and are improving the environmental potential of their fields and hedgerows under the Countryside Stewardship scheme. Visitors are encouraged to explore the meadows and wooded areas.

There are two small ponds surrounded by areas of damp ground. Bog plants thrive here in the heavy clay soil. Several beds of herbaceous plants are cleverly colour-themed, and the margins of the garden are planted to blend into the surrounding fields. At the lower end of the garden is the productive vegetable garden, and a small nursery.

On the other side of the entrance drive is a south-facing, sheltered garden. The beds at the top of this area are in full sun, and thickly planted with sedums, grasses, and other sun-loving species. As the land slopes to the stream and becomes progressively damper, the planting changes to borders of hostas, primulas, and larger shrubs, before merging into the woodland garden – an area at its best in spring.

30 Milland Farm

open	Under NGS, and by appt to buy rhododendrons
directions	SS68 10, half-way between Barnstaple and Exeter off A377 at Eggesford St, cross railway, up hill 0.75ml, R into bridleway
owners	Mr & Mrs N. Wright
address	The Old Glebe, Eggesford, Chulmleigh EX18 7QU
enquiries	T: 01769 580632
EH	House: II

NORTH

SS68 10

size	2.80h/7a
soil	Clay, pH6–6.5
altitude	150m/500ft
aspect	S–SW, AGLV
rainfall	89–201cm/35–40in
temperature	Zone D
	Nursery, by appt only, 200 varieties of rhododendrons for sale

Nigel and June Wright moved into this former rectory – a Georgian house above the Taw valley – in 1981, taking over a house and garden suffering from considerable neglect. Nigel Wright knew nothing whatever about rhododendrons, having previously gardened on chalk, but something sparked his interest, and as the garden was gradually cleared of brambles and nettles, he planted just six bushes. Nigel Wright is now one of the country's foremost authorities on the species. His private nursery supplies several hundred customers every year: some want just one special bush, others order by the hundred; all receive individual attention.

The layout of the sloping garden, with its curving lines and low stone walls, which break up the levels, was planned by June Wright, a talented botanical artist. Broad herbaceous borders near the house are backed by long yew hedges, and streams were diverted to form one long cascade, its margins densely planted with azaleas. It is crossed by two wooden bridges (Nigel's work), and flows into a large pond with a small island. The old rectory forms a focal point for the entire garden: the present building replaced a much older house, which, with 50 acres (20ha) of glebe, was a 'reward', in 1546, to the incumbent from the Norman family Reigney who had come over with William the Conqueror, and had owned the village of Eggesford since 1233. There are many veteran trees, including a grand Turkey oak – *Quercus cerris* – which is at least 170 years old. New groves have been planted, but the margins of the garden are left wild to blend with the surrounding woodland. On either side of the valley are banks of rhododendrons and azaleas, providing spectacular swathes of colour in May and June, when the garden is at its best.

31 The Old Glebe

open	Daily, except 25 Dec, am, pm
directions	SS49 17, on A3124 1ml S Torrington on Exeter road
owner	RHS
address	RHS Garden Rosemoor, Torrington EX38 8PH
enquiries	T: 01805 624067 E: rosemooradmin@ RHS.org.uk www.rhs.org.uk

NORTH

SS49 17

size	25h/60a
soil	Heavy clay, acid, and silt
altitude	40m/150ft
aspect	Level, N/S, AGLV
rainfall	89–102cm/35–40in
temperature	Zone E
NC	*Cornus, Ilex*
	Plant centre

This estate is north Devon's showpiece garden, the gift to the RHS in 1988 of one of the country's foremost gardeners, Lady Anne Palmer, whose knowledge of plants had gained her the Society's highest accolade – the Victoria Medal of Horticulture. At Rosemoor she created a first-class garden, beautifully laid out on a sloping site with a backdrop of woodland. The RHS created a brand new garden, crossing the road to the waterlogged meadows on the banks of the River Torridge. Under the direction of Major-General Rougier, experts were called in to design beds and borders, and plan the layout. RHS Rosemoor emerged from a sea of mud two years later, and has been delighting huge numbers of visitors ever since. In 2003 it was voted the South West Visitor Attraction of the Year in the South West Tourism Excellence Awards.

The centrepiece is the Formal Garden, which covers 3ha (7.5a), and is divided into different areas by hedges – there are about 1,200 yew hedging plants here! Some 2,000 rose bushes flower spectacularly for many months, despite the damp Devon air. There is a huge long border; three 'model gardens', which share a central lawn; a lovely cottage garden and a winter garden, and wonderful fruit and vegetable areas. Plant collections include species from the Southern hemisphere; alpines; foliage plants; 31 species of *Cornus*, and 37 of *Ilex*, and the cherry trees, many of which came from Collingwood 'Cherry' Ingram, a friend of Lady Anne's, who first sparked her interest in gardening. Over the years the garden has been constantly expanded and improved, so that the original and the new Rosemoor now link up via a water garden and an underpass. This area was transformed into a rock gully in 1995, and is planted with bamboos and ferns. A new arboretum adjoins the lawns of Lady Anne's garden.

32 RHS Garden Rosemoor

open	Under NGS, one Sun, Jun/Jul, pm
directions	SS49 16, 2ml S of Torrington off A386 Okehampton road, park village green
owners	Mr & Mrs M. Sampson
address	School House, Little Torrington, Torrington EX38 8PS
enquiries	T: 01805 623445

NORTH

SS49 16

size	0.3h/2/3a
soil	Heavy clay
altitude	150m/500ft
aspect	Flat, AGLV
rainfall	89–102cm/35–40in
temperature	Zone D
	Plant sales

Since 1993, rough grass surrounded by beech trees and a conifer hedge has gradually been transformed into a cottage garden. The grass and conifers have gone, and the height and number of surrounding trees have been drastically reduced, but this is still a predominantly shady garden.

The Sampsons let plants seed themselves and grow where they are happy, and there has been no formal planning. Seeds and cuttings are raised in the greenhouse and used to fill any gaps, and there are colour-themed areas. Wildlife is a priority, and it is amazing how many small ponds and areas of water have been incorporated – all a mecca for toads, frogs, and dragonflies.

The garden is packed full of plants, with herbaceous geraniums, geums, and hostas, intertwined with periwinkles and ivies. Larger shrubs and several small trees provide a framework for some of the many climbers: roses, including 'Rambling Rector' and 'Himalayan Musk', flourish, and there are at least 37 varieties of clematis. A central pergola is heavy with roses, golden hop, honeysuckle and clematis. Mrs Sampson has made up for the lack of space by growing upwards.

The garden is divided into small areas, each with its own theme or season, some sunny, most shady, but all with interesting planting. There is usually a surplus for sale, and Mr Sampson's model railway in the shed is well known to regular visitors.

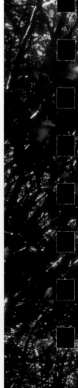

33 School House

open	Under NGS, Jun, Jul, Aug, am, pm, and by appt
directions	SS84 23, A361 Tiverton–South Molton road, R at picnic area signed Knowstone, 1.5ml to Roachill, continue to Wiston X, L, L into drive 0.25ml
owner	Anita Allen
address	Shapcott Barton, East Knowstone, South Molton EX36 4EE
enquiries	T: 01398 341664
EH	House: II*

NORTH

SS84 23

size	2h/5a of 81ha/200a
soil	Neutral
altitude	240m/800ft
aspect	S
rainfall	89–102cm+/35–40in+
temperature	Zone F
NC	*Leucanthemum* x *superbum*
	Plant sales

Originally known as East Knowstone Manor, the medieval house was home to the Shapcott family for generations, and is tucked away down a long track, surrounded by its own land of 200 acres (81ha) – a rural landscape with Exmoor in the background. Anita Allen came here in 1998, bringing with her her growing collection of shasta daisies – *Chrysanthemum* x *superbum*. Anita Allen holds the National Collection of these attractive flowers, and much of the garden is designed around them. She describes it as 'controlled chaos', and gardens to encourage wildlife as well as to enhance the setting of the manor house. A backdrop of mature trees provides necessary shelter from the prevailing winds. There are areas for different seasons – a spring meadow and a summer meadow with their own mowing regimes – and over 70 different cultivars of the shasta daisies, all carefully labelled. Anita Allen grew her first daisy when she was seven years old, as part of a cut-flower business to provide pocket-money, and from this developed an abiding interest. Holding a National Collection involves the meticulous recording of each cultivar, and the pressing of specimens. There is now one named after her – a seedling she found in the garden.

The gardens merge into the ancient woodland, where the medieval fishpond has recently been cleared out, and the dam repaired. There are plans for a bog garden here. Everything is recycled, so a fallen ash tree provides stepping stones and seats; the paths are edged with fallen branches, and stones are collected together to provide paving or walls. The latest project is a gravel garden, through which the stream runs, alongside one of the barns – which is planted with even more shasta daisies.

34 Shapcott Barton Estate

21 Mar–31 Oct, daily except Sat, am, pm	
SS47 29, off A360 Barnstaple–Bideford road, follow tourist signs, drive on R before Instow	
Christie Devon Estates	
Tapeley Park, Westleigh, Bideford. EX39 4NT	
T: 01271 342558	
House: II*	

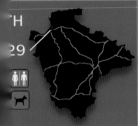

'H

29

Gardens: II	
20h/50a	
Clay	
59m/150ft	
S + W	
89–102cm/35–40in	
Zone D	
Plant sales	

The elegant, Grade II*-listed house at Tapeley Park commands panoramic views over the estuary of the Taw and Torridge rivers. Of the early 18th-century parkland, little now remains: it is the 50 acres (20ha) of gardens and terraces laid out below the house in the early 20th century that are Tapeley's finest feature. Home of the Christie family – of Glyndebourne fame – for many generations, the gardens were the work of Lady Rosamund and her architect, John Belcher. The Italian gardens lie below the house, facing south-east, the terrace walls providing shelter for many semi-tropical and tender plants. At one end of the lawn is a pond and clipped yews, leading to a summerhouse and a tunnel of clipped *Quercus ilex*. In recent years, new borders have been planted here and around the house, from which a flight of steps (formed from unused First World War gravestones – an early example of Government surplus) takes visitors to the highest point in the garden. Here is the well-maintained kitchen garden, which has an early preformed concrete greenhouse. In addition, Hector Christie has planted an organic fruit and vegetable garden alongside the drive. To the front of the house a 15m obelisk was erected to commemorate the loss of Archibald Clevland, the only son of the house, in the Crimean War. This was subsequently destroyed by lightning, and recently Hector Christie has constructed a maze from the fragments. Below, in woodlands planted with camellias and rhododendrons, a statue of Archibald's grieving mother overlooks the lake. Here, and throughout the estate, are magnificent mature trees, including many pines and conifers, and the oldest specimens of *Thuja plicata* in the country.

open	Under NGS, May–Sep, one Sun, Mon each month, pm, and by appt pm
directions	SS53 38, follow signs to Guineaford; continue on Ilfracombe road, next L at Gypsy Corner, then 2nd L, clearly signed Westcott Barton
owners	Heidi Amschwand
address	Westcott Barton, Middle MArwood, Barnstaple EX31 4EF
enquiries	T: 01271 812842
EH	House II

NORTH

SS53 38

size	0.8ha/2a
soil	Light clay
altitude	90m/300ft
aspect	SW
rainfall	76–89cm/30–35in
temperature	Zone D
	Plant sales

New owners took over Westcott Barton in October 2003, inheriting a garden lovingly created over a long period by two generations of the same family, who had farmed at Westcott for many decades. Ann Burnham, who opened the garden regularly, developed this beautiful valley setting, creating ponds, borders, and woodland walks. She had a discerning eye for good plants, and there are many unusual trees and shrubs, some well established, some newly planted. The sound of water is everywhere: the stream tumbles down the steep valley, merging below the lawn, and crossed by an ancient stone bridge that leads to the woodland walk where spring bulbs and bluebells abound.

A feature of the garden is the number of trellis frames supporting a variety of climbers, mainly clematis, that thrive in the sheltered valley. Roses cover an old stone arch and a small arbour, and there is a good mix of herbaceous plants in the many borders. The garden has been extended up the valley, with a young pleached lime walk taking shape. The farmhouse dates from the 13th century, and across the yard are a range of stone barns, now used for social functions; a huge water-wheel that once powered the various implements still housed in the barn, and an ancient tithe barn higher up the lane. This is one of Devon's hidden gems, largely untouched by time.

36 Westcott Barton

open	May–Oct, daily except Tue, am, pm, and by appt all year
directions	SS44 01, from Halwill Junction take Black Torrington road; R at sign; 0.5ml L at sign
owners	Mrs Aileen Birks & Mr Michael Gilmore
address	Winsford Walled Garden, Halwill Junction EX21 5XT
enquiries	T: 01409 221477 E: muddywellies@ winsfordwalledgarden. freeserve.co.uk www.winsfordwalled garden.freeserve.co.uk

NORTH

SS44 01

size	0.5h/1a
soil	Neutral/acid
altitude	130m/450ft
aspect	Level
rainfall	89–102cm/35–40in
temperature	Zone E

It is remarkable how much two dedicated gardeners can achieve in a very short time, if they have determination – and a digger. In 1999, when Michael Gilmore and his mother, Aileen Birks, bought the former walled garden of the now-demolished Winsford Towers, it was derelict; the glasshouses, where they survived at all, were in ruins. Little was left of the original garden, constructed in 1883, except the walls, which in themselves provide insufficient shelter from the strong winds that cross this flat part of Devon. The digger carried out essential clearance work, and then the planning began. There are now over 2,000 different plants in carefully designed beds. Each bed has a backbone of shrubs or small trees, including *Cornus*, *Laburnum*, *Pittosporum*, *Pinus*, *Cedrus*, *Michelia*, and *Hoheria* – designed both to act as a windbreak, and in future to provide some shade. Many exotics are doing very well, and the lush growth everywhere is evidence of a programme of manuring, watering, and constant attention. The space has been cleverly broken up, and apart from restoring the surviving glasshouses, the owners have avoided the more common 'restored Victorian walled garden' approach. Michaelmas daisies are grown as groundcover surrounding a stone column; thymes grow in ornate compost bins, and a rescued flight of slate steps has water trickling down it into a pond – one of the water reservoirs for the garden. In the glasshouses are a large collection of unusual *Canna*, *Hedychium*, *Musa*, *Alocassia*, *Colocassia*, and *Curcuma* plants, which flourish in the warm, moist atmosphere. New developments are still being planned, so regular visitors will enjoy watching progress.

37 Winsford Walled Garden

Exeter was an early Celtic settlement, and became Isca Dumnoniorum, a fortified outpost of the Roman Empire, in about 50–55AD. In the predominantly rural area of mid-Devon, the city grew in prosperity during the Middle Ages thanks to the wool trade, and in particular the manufacture of serge cloth. It became the administrative centre of the county in 1050, when Bishop Leofric transferred the seat of the bishopric to Exeter from Crediton, the geographical centre and meeting point of trade routes from Barnstaple, Okehampton, and Tiverton. Exeter Cathedral was begun on the site of the Roman baths, using stone from the historic quarry at Beer, as well as other Devon quarries. The nave, choir, and sanctuary can boast the longest uninterrupted example of Gothic vaulting in the world. Exeter's Guildhall (c.1330) is held to be the oldest municipal building in the country, and the Custom House (1681) and Tuckers' Hall (1471), originally the Hall of the Weavers, Fullers, and Shearmen, stand as monuments to the prosperity that Exeter enjoyed from the profits of the wool trade until the 18th century. The Elizabethan canal – the first in the country to use pound locks – enhanced Exeter's trade as a port.

John Heathcoat moved his lace-making business to a former wool mill in Tiverton. His grandson, John Heathcoat-Amory, built **Knightshayes Court** (43) on land overlooking the family lace factory. This factory was to become the largest of its kind in the world.

Having sustained extensive bomb damage from the 'Baedeker raids' of the Second World War, parts of Exeter city centre had to be redeveloped, but there are plenty of old buildings left, and many squares and public parks planted with trees and shrubs: even the multi-storey car-park overlooking the river is treated as a hanging garden. Indeed, modern Exeter could well claim to be called a garden city, so well planted are its streets and suburbs.

The River Exe rises on Exmoor in the north, flowing through a beautiful wooded valley before it broadens below

3 *MID*

Tiverton on its way to the sea. Here, on the fertile ground, are the gardens of **Killerton** (42), **Sherwood** (48), and **Shobrooke** (49), some of the finest in mid-Devon. John Veitch, having designed the gardens at Killerton, set up his world-famous nursery at Budlake nearby, under the patronage of Sir Thomas Acland, in 1808. The business moved to Mount Radford,

Exeter, in 1832, and by 1853 had established a London branch, The Royal Exotic Nurseries. The firm supplied trees for the arboretum at **Streatham Hall** – now the University Campus – where visitors can enjoy a Sculpture Walk in the grounds. The Exeter firm of Veitch was managed by members of the family until 1969, when it was sold.

open	Under NGS, Apr–Sep, some Tue, Wed, Sun, pm, and by appt
directions	SX91 84, 1ml off A38 Exeter–Plymouth road, L at Kennford Services, follow signs for Kenn, 1st R in village
owners	Mr & Mrs J. Tremlett
address	Bickham House, Kenn, Exeter EX6 7XL
enquiries	T: 01392 832671
EH	House: II*

MID

SX91 84

size	2.8h/7a
soil	Slightly acid
altitude	120m/400ft
aspect	E, AGLV
rainfall	76–89cm/30–35in
temperature	Zone F
	Plant sales

This beautiful, 17th-century house, set in seven acres (2.8ha) of gardens, is situated in the seclusion of a wooded valley. It is still occupied by descendants of the family that built it – although things have changed since the days when there were 12 indoor staff and at least six gardeners. The Tremletts began gardening seriously at Bickham in 1967, and opened to the public in 1993. The herbaceous borders; the planting of rhododendrons in the woodland; the addition of many fine trees, and the digging of a one-acre (0.4ha) lake at the lowest point in the garden below the house, are all their work. Much careful thought has gone into the design and planting, from the plantation of trees beyond the entrance gates, to the delightful small pond outside the walled garden. This area has been completely revolutionized, and is Julia Tremlett's particular pride: she divided it up parterre-fashion, with a potager and herb garden, some lawn, flowerbeds planted with many shrub roses, and a vegetable plot. A central path leads to the orchard and a small arboretum beyond, where a timber summerhouse forms a focal point. It is pleasant to sit here and enjoy the views of the rest of the garden. Behind the house is a formal garden: a pond planted with arum lilies and box-edged beds have taken the place of what was previously a dull yard. The veranda affords protection to a host of climbers and shrubs, which are allowed to form blocks of foliage, and to the south side of the house a Victorian conservatory houses a collection of tender plants.

38 Bickham House

open	Under NGS, Apr–May, some Sat, Sun, am, pm, and by appt
directions	SX88 86, from A 30 pass through Ide to Dunchideock, L to Lord Haldon hotel, 1st L past hotel entrance
owners	Mr & Mrs J.E. Phythian
address	Haldon Grange, Dunchideock, Exeter EX6 7YE
enquiries	T: 01392 832349 E: tphythian@ tinyworld.co.uk

MID

SX88 86

P

♿

size	3.2ha/8a
soil	Acid
altitude	100m/350ft
aspect	W, AGLV
rainfall	89–102cm/35–40in
temperature	Zone F
	Plant sales

Haldon House was a casualty of the First World War. Begun in 1717, and greatly extended by the Palk family, later the Lords Haldon, it was last occupied by the Bannatynes, whose only son was killed in 1916, a year after his father had died. In 1919 the estate was put on the market, and eventually sold piece-meal, the house being demolished in 1925. Only one wing of the building survives, as the present Lord Haldon Hotel. The grounds of a new house, Haldon Grange, are the former pleasure-gardens of the original house, and cover eight acres (3.2ha). They contain two 'champions' – *Cupressus lusitanica* 'Glauca Pendula' and *Pinus wallichiana* – the largest recorded of their kind in the country – and the Haldon Oak, planted in 1730. Even without the display of towering rhododendrons and banks of azaleas, this garden would be memorable for its trees alone. A large weeping beech overhangs the drive, a *Davidia* flutters its 'handkerchiefs', and there are many rare pines and conifers, some dating from the mid-19th century. The present owners, who have been here since 1981, and at one time ran a success-ful nursery, have planted a spinney of unusual trees in the area known as Mount Pleasant, from which visitors can enjoy fine views across the valley of the Exe to Exeter. A tributary of the River Kenn runs through the garden, and has been dammed to form a large pond. Here, a stone seat commemorates Neville Randall, who lived at Haldon Grange from 1940 until his death in 1956, and planned the structure and planted many of the shrubs. The present owners have planted borders of rhododendrons and azaleas, and other shrubs and trees.

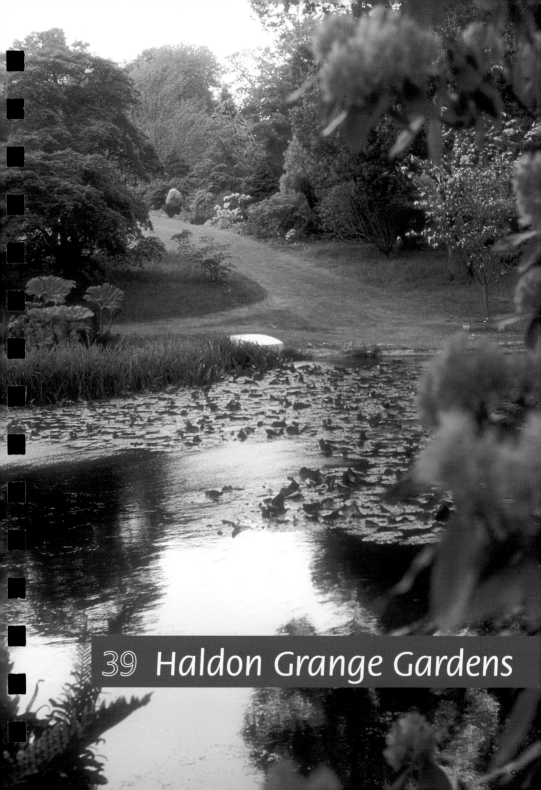

39 Haldon Grange Gardens

open	Apr–end Sep, Thur, Fri, Sat, am, pm, and groups by appt
directions	ST04 15, M5 Junction 27, signs for Minnows campsite, 300yd up hill
owners	Mr Hughes-Jones & Mrs Proud
address	Holbrook Garden, Sampford Shrubs, Sampford Peverell, Tiverton EX16 7EN
enquiries	T: 01884 821164 www.samshrub.co.uk

MID

ST04 15

size	0.8h/2a
soil	Heavy clay, pH6
altitude	120m/400ft
aspect	S, AGLV
rainfall	91–102cm/36–40in
temperature	Zone E
NC	*Heleniums*
	Nursery

It is difficult to know where the nursery ends and the garden begins, so seamlessly do they merge. Begun as a business in 1984, the gardens are an eye-opener: they work harmoniously with nature by encouraging natural pest controls and ecological planting. The house has all but disappeared under a drapery of climbers, and the gardens themselves are lush with healthy plants. Huge clumps of hostas are almost entirely free of slug damage: the secret is to encourage rove beetles, which helpfully live off slugs' eggs, and there is even one that eats snails' innards! Aphids are regarded as helpful because they are a magnet for many welcome predators, and only roses that will succeed without spraying are grown. There is a surprisingly wide range. Anyone who lacks the courage or conviction to switch to organic gardening needs only to visit Holbrook Garden and talk to the owners to be converted. New ideas are constantly being tried out, and the couple usually return home with new plants after travelling. For example, a German holiday has resulted in a dry bed covered in a shingle mulch, planted with swathes of *Verbena bonariensis*, intermixed with perennial yellow daisies. There is something of interest to be seen at all times of the year, with some borders designed to be particularly good in late summer and early autumn. The garden is home to the National Collection of *Heleniums*.

40 Holbrook Garden

open	Apr–Sep, some Sun; Bank Holiday Mon, pm, and by appt
directions	ST01 07, from Cullompton town centre turn up by Manor House Hotel, L Langlands Rd, R at T junction; 300yd R, beyond rugby club
owners	Mrs M.B. Disney
address	Kia-Ora Farm, Knowle Lane, Cullompton EX15 1PS
enquiries	T: 01884 32347 www.kia-orafarm.co.uk

MID

ST01 07

P P₊

size	4h/10a landscaped gardens and lakes
soil	Medium loam and clay
altitude	60m/200ft
aspect	Level
rainfall	76–89cm/30–35in
temperature	Zone F
	Plant sales

Mary Disney is a compulsive gardener: the original small plot of just 0.75 acre (0.3ha) around the house has gradually developed outwards, so that the garden has grown in sections. It now extends to 4.5 acres (1.8ha), and planning permission was required when she took in the furthest field. The farm owes its unusual name to its original owners, who came from New Zealand.

Mrs Disney loves colour, and her flowerbeds are overflowing with pink and red roses; tall spires of lupins; snapdragons, and poppies, with unclipped escallonia hedges as a backdrop and windbreak. Kia-Ora Farm is situated on underlying clay, so there is an abundance of water to be tapped into, and in recent years a series of ponds has been excavated, which are now home to a large population of ducks and wildfowl that wander around the gardens at will.

Children are particularly welcome at Kia-Ora Farm, and the original Three Bears garden delights Mrs Disney's own grandchildren. The most recent addition is a series of gardens based on nursery rhymes, which should be a particular boon for visitors with young children to amuse.

41 Kia-Ora Farm

<table>
<tr><td>open</td><td>Daily, am, pm</td></tr>
<tr><td>directions</td><td>SS97 00, B3181 Exeter to Cullompton, 7ml fork L, follow NT signs</td></tr>
<tr><td>owner</td><td>NT</td></tr>
<tr><td>address</td><td>Killerton, Broadclyst, EX5 3LE</td></tr>
<tr><td>enquiries</td><td>T: 01392 881345
E: killerton@nationaltrust.org.uk
www.nationaltrust.org.uk</td></tr>
<tr><td>EH</td><td>House: II*</td></tr>
</table>

MID

SS97 00

size	8h/20a
soil	Acid, sandy loam
altitude	40–90m/150–300ft
aspect	S
rainfall	76–89cm/30–35in
temperature	Zone F
	Plant centre

Killerton House was built in 1779, and altered in the late 1890s. Parkland stretches beyond the ha-ha; broad carriage drives connect the house to the stables, and meander through the park. But what makes Killerton exceptional is the quality of the planting throughout the 20 acres (8ha) of grounds.

The garden was originally laid out by Veitch in the late 18th century, employed by Sir Thomas Acland as his agent for his estates. He encouraged him to set up a nursery close to Killerton. Veitch employed plant-hunters to travel the world for unusual specimens, and some were planted at Killerton. The *Sequoiadendron giganteum* was introduced in 1853, and planted at Killerton in 1858, an original introduction by William Lobb. There are groves of fine magnolias, many originally from Veitch, and two tulip trees, believed to be the tallest specimens in the country. Thick banks of mature rhododendrons and camellias are set against a backdrop of trees, and an avenue of old beeches leads to the woodland, which contains many fine specimen trees. The terrace, with its beautifully kept herbaceous borders, dates from about 1900.

42 Killerton Garden

open	Mid-Mar–Nov, daily, am, pm
directions	SS96 15, A396 Tiverton–Bampton, follow NT signs
owner	NT
address	Knightshayes Court, Bolham, Tiverton EX16 7RQ
enquiries	T: 01884 254665 E: knightshayes@ nationaltrust.or.uk www.nationaltrust. or.uk
EH	House: I

MID

SS96 15

P P+ ♿ 👫
🍴 📖 🛍️ 🐕   ♨

EH	Gardens: II*
size	20h/50a
soil	Devon marl; 4.5–6.5pH
altitude	122–152m/400–500ft
aspect	S + W, AGLV
rainfall	89–102cm/35–40in
temperature	Zone E
	Plant centre

Knightshayes Court was begun in the late 1860s by John Heathcoat, on a site with a fine view over Tiverton and his own successful lace factory. The garden was laid out by Edward Kemp, a garden writer and landscape designer, on former farmland. Many of the magnificent trees were planted at this time, as were most of the yew hedges – to which, in 1920, Sir Ian Heathcoat-Amory added the topiary hounds everlastingly chasing a yew fox. It was the next generation – Sir John and his wife, Joyce, Lady Amory – who developed the gardens as we see them today, calling upon the services of some of the foremost horticultural experts of the day – Graham Stuart Thomas, Lanning Roper who helped with the pool garden, and Sir Eric Savill from Windsor Great Park. Over their long lives the Amorys became acknowledged experts, and both were awarded the Victoria Medal of Honour by the RHS. They described Knightshayes as a 'garden in the wood', rather than a woodland garden.

Spring is a time of bulbs and flowering cherries, and the garden is justly famed for its camellias, of which there are a huge number, together with many species rhododendrons. Summer sees good herbaceous planting, and autumn colour can be spectacular in the wide variety of trees and shrubs. The garden, which covers 50 acres (20ha), seems to have no end, stretching along the main drive into the surrounding woodland, where there are a number of good walks, and down the hillside to a pond. There is also the newly restored kitchen garden to see. Small, intimate areas combine with grand designs, and no detail is overlooked, thanks mainly to Michael Hickson, the former head gardener, who began working at Knightshayes for the Amorys in 1963, and continued for 30 years after the property passed to the National Trust in 1973.

43 Knightshayes Gardens

MID

ST09 12

size	0.4ha/1a
soil	Heavy clay, neutral to acid
altitude	120m/400ft
aspect	Level
rainfall	76–89cm/35–40in
temperature	Zone F
NC	*Dierama* species
	Plant sales

There was very little planting at Little Southey when Stuart and Diane Rowe moved here in 1984 with their family and animals – just a few simple beds laid out in the 1960s, and a preponderance of conifers. And the underlying heavy clay was not encouraging. Drainage was improved, and the first year was spent breaking up the clay soil. Manure from their own horses helped greatly, and now the soil is friable and healthy, although they are still adding lashings of compost. Many of the conifers were removed, and groups of trees were planted – some for shelter, some to provide autumn colour, such as *Eucryphia*, *Sorbus* and *Acer*, with belts of shrubs weaving through them. Throughout the garden, bulbs have been planted and allowed to naturalize – the central lawn is not mowed until the end of July, and now contains a wide variety of grasses, wild flowers and early bulbs. Beyond is the orchard of old cider apple trees, the lone survivor in the hamlet of Northcott, which at one time was renowned for its orchards.

Around the house and terrace the emphasis is on summer planting, but elsewhere the borders are a mixture of herbaceous subjects intermingled with shrubs, so there is always something of interest. The NCCPG National Collection of *Dierama* is in a special bed beyond the main lawn, but *Dieramas* are also planted in the borders, particularly in the sheltered gravel area close to the former farmhouse, which dates from the 17th century. This is a very peaceful garden, attracting large numbers of birds that nest everywhere, including the outhouses and barns, and have been known to take up residence in discarded flowerpots.

44 Little Southey

open	Apr–Sep, some Sat/Sun, am, pm, and by appt
directions	ST14 13, 0.5ml S of Hemyock, turn up by pump, drive near top of hill on L
owners	Mr & Mrs J. Ward
address	Newton Farm, Hemyock, Cullompton EX15 3QS
enquiries	T: 01823 680410

MID

ST14 13

size	2.4h/6a
soil	Neutral/acid
altitude	240m/800ft
aspect	Level plateau
rainfall	76–89cm/30–35in
temperature	Zone F
NC	*Gentians, Rhodohypoxis*
	Plant sales; wholesale nursery

Wind is a considerable problem here, high on the Blackdown Hills, so shelterbelts are essential. The property was originally a farm, and the house is thought to date from about 1525, when a marriage was recorded between two families who still live nearby. By 1984, when the Wards moved in, the house, buildings, and land were semi-derelict, and the first task was to make the house habitable once again. Work is still in progress on the other buildings. The Wards are enthusiastic plantsmen, and have set up a specialist wholesale nursery in and around the farmyard, where over 120 different varieties of gentians create carpets of blue flowers in the autumn. There are also two beds of these plants by the house. The flat, windswept site is surrounded by a shelterbelt, and has been developed with a large maze of beech – the original yew had to be replaced as it didn't like the underlying clinker – broad herbaceous borders planted with large perennials, a tunnel of hornbeam trained over a redundant polythene-tunnel frame, and areas devoted to *Hemerocallis*, *Iris ensata*, and *I. Siberica*, for which a new garden is planned beyond the poplar hedge. One of the first areas to be planted was a bed of dwarf conifers and heathers close to the house: the Tasmanian strawberry pine – *Podocarpus alpinus* – a rarity in this country, is flourishing here. A new area being developed is the old drove-road, leading to Hemyock Common, which is sheltered by ancient hedgerows and contains a dew-pond.

45 Newton Farm

open	May–Oct, some Sat, Sun, am, pm, and by appt
directions	ST14 11, 7ml N Honiton, through Dunkeswell towards Hemyock as far as Gypsy X, then follow signs on NGS dates; or phone/write for detailed directions
owners	Mr & Mrs B. Carver
address	Pikes Cottage, Madford, Hemyock EX15 3QZ
enquiries	T: 01823 680345

MID

ST14 11

size	2.4h/6a
soil	Greensand, stony, acid
altitude	180–210m/600–700ft
aspect	W, AONB
rainfall	89–102cm/35–40in
temperature	Zone F
	Plant sales

Some people sit back when they retire, and plan leisurely activities. Not so the Carvers, who could not wait to get started on the garden of their new property, deep in the countryside of the Blackdown Hills. The Carvers moved to Pikes Cottage in 1990, bringing with them two vans loaded with plants from their Hertfordshire garden. Among this collection were the box cuttings taken from Box Hill in Surrey, which now form the edges to the herb garden by the 17th-century cottage. Not content with a small area of garden around the cottage, leaving the rest of the 19 acres (7.6ha) to woodland, the Carvers incorporated most of the land, some of it as managed woodland. The lawn was created by regular mowing, and the large pond was excavated to take advantage of a naturally damp area. At the top of the lawn is a circle of conifers underplanted with heathers, harebells, and thymes. Brian Carver is particularly interested in conifers, and has planted many rare varieties. The idea for a new arboretum developed from an existing oak tree, now the centre of a 'Quercus circus', with five seats, hedges, and radiating paths. From here there are fine views over the countryside, and in spring the bluebells flower abundantly. Closer to the house are a sensory garden, a scree area, an Antipodean corner … and a lovely sense of peace.

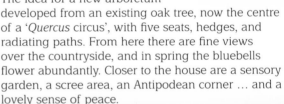

46 Pikes Cottage

open	Early Apr–early Oct, daily except Sat, am, pm
directions	SX96 83, signed off A379 Exeter–Torbay, entrance Kenton village
owners	Earl & Countess of Devon
address	Powderham Castle, Kenton EX6 8JQ
enquiries	T: 01626 890243 E: castle@powderham. co.uk
EH	House: I

MID

SX96 83

EH	Grounds: II*
size	2.4h/6a, in large estate
soil	Neutral loam
altitude	15m/50ft
aspect	S + E, AGLV
rainfall	76–89cm/30–35in
temperature	Zone F
	Plant centre

Situated on the west bank of the Exe estuary, Powderham has been home to the Courtenay family since 1325, when it formed part of the dowry of Lady Margaret de Bohun at her marriage with Hugh Courtenay, Second Earl of Devon. In recent times it has been necessary to run the castle along commercial lines, but it is still basically a family home. The estate covers some 3,700 acres (1,500ha) of beautiful Devon countryside, reaching up to the surrounding hills, and is managed along traditional lines. In the grounds is a triangular Belvedere Tower, similar to Haldon Belvedere, built to take advantage of the views of the parkland and estuary. Around the castle is the ancient deer park – a rare survivor that still maintains a herd of deer. Dotted about are many ancient trees – the hallmark of a great estate – and belts of woodland. Below the castle is a large lake, home to a wide variety of wildfowl.

The terrace to the front of the castle has been planted with a formal rose garden and lawns. It is here that Timothy the tortoise has his home: he was given to the Earl of Devon's great-grandmother in 1892, and moved to Powderham in 1935.

In spring, drifts of daffodils line the drives, and the American garden with its many rhododendrons is a beautiful sight.

47 Powderham Castle

open	All year, Sun pm, and by appt
directions	SX96 85, 2ml SE Crediton off Exeter road, signed Sherwood
owners	Sir John & Lady Quicke
address	Sherwood, Newton St Cyres, Exeter EX5 5BT
enquiries	T: 01392 851216

MID

SX96 85

size	6h/14a
soil	Culm measures, clay
altitude	120m/400ft
aspect	N + S, AGLV
rainfall	63–70cm/25–30in
temperature	Zone E
NC	Knaphill azaleas, *Magnolias*

Buried deep in wooded country, down a long, winding lane, lies the beautiful estate of Sherwood. It has been owned by only two couples, both expert gardeners. The house was built in 1907 for Adrian Cave, to designs by his cousin Walter, in the Arts and Crafts style fashionable at the time. It was Adrian and his wife Chrissie Cave who began the development of the magnificent gardens that now extend from the entrance gates up to, and well beyond the house. Several steep valleys converge on the site, all with mature tree canopy thinned to admit light, and all richly planted.

The present owner moved from Newton St Cyres in 1968, bringing with him some of his collection of rhododendrons. Sir John Quicke is extremely knowledgeable, and is a connoisseur of fine plants, especially rhododendrons, azaleas, and magnolias, of which he has planted hundreds. His wife, Prue, has a keen sense of colour and design, and together they have brought Sherwood gardens to a state of near perfection. At all times of the year there is something to be seen, from banks of wild daffodils and early magnolias, the heather bank by the house, and drifts of Knaphill azaleas – which Sir John considers are undervalued at present – through to glorious autumn colour from the many trees and shrubs. More recently, Sir John has begun collecting *Berberis*, which are planted at the top of the garden by the perimeter fence (against the deer). There is always some new project, and the current scheme is to clear banks of laurel at the lower end of the garden to make way for more acers, magnolias, and rhododendrons – although Sir John considers that the rainfall is insufficient for them.

open	Under NGS, Apr–Jun, some Sat, pm, and by appt. Park open daily
directions	SX85 01, 1ml NE Crediton on A3072 Tiverton road, turn at lodge
owners	Dr & Mrs J.R. Shelley
address	Shobrooke Park, Crediton EX17 1DG
enquiries	T: 01363 775153 www.shobrookepark.com

MID

SX85 01

EH	Gardens: II
size	7h/17a
soil	Red culm, silty
altitude	60–90m/200–300ft
aspect	S
rainfall	89–102cm/35–40in
temperature	Zone E
	Plant centre

Shobrooke Park is the perfect small estate, with park-land and beautiful gardens complemented by the listed Portland stonework. From the terrace, the view stretches across the parkland to three lakes, spanned by the arched stone bridge, where an amphitheatre was constructed in 2000; or across to the (listed) shell seat built as a focal point on the skyline. The long avenue of venerable lime trees leads from the higher entrance gates to the site of the original house, down by the cricket pitch. The house – destroyed by fire in 1945 – was built in 1845, when the gardens were laid out, making copious use of Portland stone for the balustrading; several sets of fine gate piers; the sundial and fountain gardens, and the two shell seats.

Several decades of neglect followed the loss of the house, until the present owner's mother, Mrs Dorothy Shelley, moved back in 1968, built herself a bungalow on the terrace, and began, almost single-handedly, to rescue the former gardens. Dr and Mrs Shelley have carried on the long process, with the help of a number of people, and in recent years the gardens have re-emerged more splendid than ever. Vast numbers of trees have been planted throughout the estate, and the laurel walk re-created. The original rose garden had completely disappeared, and was started afresh in 1996. It is a stunning success, particularly in early June, with festoons of roses supported on ropes and chains; columns of climbers, and beds full of scented bushes. In early spring, daffodils are followed by a vivid carpet of bluebells under the trees, setting off the ca-mellias and rhododendrons, some of which are survivors from the original garden.

49 Shobrooke Park Gardens

MID

SS94 15

size	1.7h/4a
soil	Culm measures
altitude	100m/250ft
aspect	E slope, AGLV
rainfall	89–102cm/35–40in
temperature	Zone D
	Plant sales

Given the beautiful site, it is easy to understand the philosophy of its owner, Dr Haig, that nature should be left to herself, and encouraged to benefit the human race. From his Edwardian house, the land falls steeply to the banks of the Exe, here a broad and normally placid river. Mature trees line the banks and the side of the valley: the atmosphere is one of complete peace. A garden in the conventional sense would be completely inappropriate. Broad grass paths traverse the slopes, one leading to the Stage – a small, circular area dominated by an oak tree reckoned to be 200 years old. There are two viewing areas; wild-flower beds; herb borders, and a riverbank walk. Everything is planned to encourage wildlife, and there are nesting boxes everywhere, attracting a growing variety of birds each year. Slates placed at intervals on the ground provide a refuge for glow-worms, snakes, and lizards. Over 30 varieties of butterfly have been recorded, and there is an abundance of frogs and toads, newts and dragonflies. Young trees are encouraged; there are several wild orchids, and abundant wild flowers throughout the year. This is a place for peace and tranquility, somewhere to sit and think and, as the owner says, 'gain refreshment and healing in an increasingly pressured world'. Dr Haig has been considerably cheered that, after many years of preaching the healing qualities of plants and in particular, trees, he has at long last been taken seriously, and the NHS is now advising hospitals to plant trees for the benefit of patients and staff, stating that 'patients recovering from surgery who can see trees need less medication and have faster recovery times'.

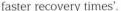

50 Spillifords Wildlife Garden

PINK PURSLANE
(...ra sibirica)

open	2nd Sun Jul–2nd Thur Sep, Sun, Bank Holiday Mon, Tue, Wed, Thu, pm
directions	SX87 78, tourist signs from A38 and A380
owner	Lord Clifford
address	The Estate Office, Ugbrooke House, Chudleigh TQ13 0AD
enquiries	T: 01626 852179
EH	House: I

MID

SX87 78

EH	Gardens: II*
size	2.4h/6a
soil	Neutral, shillet and clay
altitude	60m/200ft
aspect	SW + S, AGLV
rainfall	102–114cm/40–45in
temperature	Zone D

This beautiful estate lies in a secluded valley, and takes its name from the Ug Brook, dammed by 'Capability' Brown in the early 1770s to form two large lakes. These now dominate the view from the house across parkland with some venerable trees, to the woodland on the far side, much of it dating from Brown's time. The house, which has been lived in by the Cliffords since the 16th century, dates from Tudor times, but was extended and remodelled by Robert Adam in the 1760s: his work can be seen in the chapel wing. The window surrounds and crenellations are the result of mid-19th-century alterations.

In recent years the present Lady Clifford and the talented head gardener have created several charming garden areas close to the house. A small courtyard has been transformed into a shady Spanish garden, and leads to the fernery. Formal parterre planting enhances the 18th-century orangery on the land above the house, and there are some fine specimen trees on the highest ground. Against the shelter of a stone wall, a new rose garden has been planted, overlooking the terrace. This is separated from the parkland by a ha-ha and, as well as a knot garden planted in the 1940s, contains a timber gazebo, formal beds, and four clipped, standard hollies. More natural planting, including banks of hydrangeas, borders the walks down to, and around, the lake. The lakeside walk is about a mile long, and leads to the Watersplash.

51 Ugbrooke Park

open	Under NGS, and by appt
directions	SS80 14, on B3137 Tiverton–South Moltonroad, 3ml W Tiverton, 10yd W of 30mph sign at white gate
owners	Mrs T. Matheson
address	Withleigh Farm, Withleigh, Tiverton EX16 8JG
enquiries	T: 01884 253853

MID

SS80 14

P

size	0.8h/2a
soil	Heavy clay
altitude	180m/600ft
aspect	SW
rainfall	89–102cm/35–40in
temperature	Zone E

Faced with a site such as this, most gardeners would not even have made a start, but the owner, Mrs Tam Matheson, carried on for over 20 years, to create a lovely country garden. The fields below the farmhouse were soggy, with poorly drained, sticky clay, and sloped steeply to an insignificant stream, now widened and enlarged with three silt pools. Winds whistle up the valley. The area was full of buttercups, but instead of being condemned as weeds, these were left undisturbed to produce a sheet of brilliant golden flowers in spring. The philosophy of this garden is to try to work with, rather than against, nature, and this area now forms a safe haven for the common spotted orchid, which is happily cohabiting with the buttercups in increasing numbers. A shelterbelt and small arboretum were planted on the opposite hillside, and here rhododendrons, azaleas, and summer-flowering shrubs form a wonderful display. Emerging from a copse of alder is a stream, the margins of which were densely planted, only to be eroded by yearly floods and underground springs, which caused the banks to collapse. The area had to be rebuilt, and the stream is now lined with old railway sleepers. Other features include the main arched bridge (right), the smaller bridge, and the graceful gazebo – a recent addition overlooking the main pond. After much research over the years – including a visit to the Victoria & Albert Museum – these were designed by Mrs Matheson, and constructed by local craftsman John Tucker. Around the house are smaller borders and beds, and a new 'sunken garden'.

52 Withleigh Farm

East Devon was a distinct area even before it was defined by the construction of the M5. The underlying granite that influences the rest of Devon and Cornwall here gives way to soft red sandstone, which merges into chalk at the furthest limits around Beer and Axminster. The ancient limestone quarries at Beer, which had been worked for over 2,000 years before production ended in the 1920s, have provided stone for Exeter, Winchester, and St Paul's Cathedrals, Westminster Abbey and the Tower of London, among other famous landmarks. Contours in the landscape are noticeably softer: there is no bleak moorland, and no wild coastline. This is the country of pretty thatched cottages and picturesque villages. The mild climate and attractive landscape encouraged the gentry to settle here and build large estates: **Bicton** (53, 54), **Cadhay** (57), and **Escot** (59) are good examples. There are large tracts of sandy soil, especially around Woodbury Common, and to the east the high ridges contain a wealth of prehistoric remains. The Romans came here briefly, ending one of their roads at Axminster.

Tourism has long provided prosperity for the area, and Exmouth, with its graceful Georgian houses, claims to be one of the first of the many Devon seaside resorts. Sidmouth's prosperity is the legacy of tourism in an age when the fashion for Grand Tours around continental Europe was frustrated by the Napoleonic wars. The construction of Brunel's Great Western Railway, which reached Exeter in the early 1840s, boosted the tourist industry in the southern coastal resorts. Sidmouth has never looked back from the

4 EAST

days when its popularity was given royal approval: in 1820 the Duke and Duchess of Kent came here with their infant daughter, who would become Queen Victoria. With its Regency terraces and imposing hotels, this is a seaside resort *par excellence*, and its floral displays, at **Connaught Gardens** and in the flowering baskets on balconies, are stunning.

127

open	Mar–Oct, daily; Nov–Feb, Mon–Fri, am, pm
directions	SY07 86, 3ml N Budleigh Salterton, B3178, use Sidmouth Lodge entrance
owners	Bicton College
address	Bicton College, East Budleigh EX9 7BY
enquiries	T: 01395 562400 E: pechampion@ bicton.ac.uk
EH	House: II

EH	Gardens: I
size	57h/150a, including parkland
soil	Sandy loam on pebble bed
altitude	45m/150ft
aspect	Level, AONB
rainfall	89–102cm/35–40in
temperature	Zone F
NC	*Agapanthus, Pittosporum*
	Nursery

The house of the Rolle family, once the hub of their vast Devon estates, is now a land-based college. Completed *c.*1800, to designs by James Wyatt, it was surrounded by gracious grounds and fine woodlands. The somewhat severe appearance of the house today is the result of remodelling in 1908.

Although in divided ownership (Bicton Botanical Gardens, and Bicton Arena), most of the grounds survive. The famous avenue of monkey-puzzle trees leading to the house was planted in 1842: each tree grows on an earth mound to ensure good drainage. The formal gardens – **Bicton Park Botanical Gardens** (54) – are on the far side of the lake, but the College retains the renowned arboretum, begun *c.*1830 for Lord John Rolle, and continued by succeeding generations. There is a strong Veitch connection, with the former nursery supplying many of the trees and shrubs, which were planted by genus. The groves of limes, prunus, and many magnolias are at their best in the spring.

The former kitchen gardens are utilized by the College as a nursery and teaching area. The Yard garden has its own microclimate, in which many tender plants flourish. The greenhouses and beautifully planted trial beds, maintained by the students, lie beyond. There is great variety here, from 'parks department' bedding schemes and beds of grasses, to roses and herbaceous plants. The College holds the National Collections of *Agapanthus* and *Pittosporum*, and also has a comprehensive collection of bamboos. A more intimate walled garden is planted with many tender perennials, and beyond, the woodland extends to the stream and otter pool. There is a camellia walk along the higher wall.

53 Bicton College Gardens & Arboretum

open	Daily, except 25 Dec, am, pm
directions	SY06 86, 3ml N Budleigh Salterton, B3178, use Sidmouth Lodge entrance on Sidmouth road
owners	Mr & Mrs S. Lister
address	Bicton Park Botanical Gardens, East Budleigh EX9 7BS
enquiries	T: 01395 568465 www.bictongardens.co.uk

EAST

SY06 86

EH	Gardens: I
size	25.5h/63a
soil	Sandy loam, pebble base
altitude	45m/150ft
aspect	S + E, AONB
rainfall	89–102cm/35–40in
temperature	Zone F
	Plant centre

It is almost impossible to see the mansion from these, the formal gardens, which were laid out from the mid-18th century onwards. The 'Italian' gardens – on a slope falling to a formal rectangular pond with a fountain, flanked on three sides by a canal – are the earliest, dating from 1735. Their design has been attributed to André Le Notre, who also designed gardens at Versailles. High retaining banks on the far side divide to form an axial view to the obelisk (1747). Overlooking the gardens is the Orangery, now a restaurant. Other 19th-century features include a shell house, ice-house, hermitage, American garden, and mausoleum; but the most famous is the glass palm house. At 68ft (21m) long, it is smaller than one might expect, but with wonderful curves: it is thought to pre-date its larger relative at Kew by some 20 years. There are about 18,000 overlapping panes of glass in the structure, which was a birthday present for Lady Louisa Rolle from her husband, Lord Rolle, at a time when the window-tax was still in force. The large lake was constructed by French prisoners of war in 1812. The house is on the far side.

The gardens, which include the famous pinetum, have had a chequered history since the house was leased separately to Devon County Council in 1946. They were first opened to the public in 1963, and later developed as a tourist attraction with a narrow-gauge railway, café, and museum of country life. After a period of decline, the present owners took over in 1998, and have revived the Grade I listed park, with its magnificent trees. Garden visitors are advised to go in spring or early summer, avoiding peak holiday periods when the other attractions are busy with family parties. (See also Bicton College Gardens & Arboretum, 53.)

54 Bicton Park Botanical Gardens

open	Under NGS, Jun, some Wed, Sat, Sun, pm
directions	SY13 91, park in free car-park in Sidbury; walk up lane; 1st entrance beyond new housing
owners	Mr & Mrs A. Softly
address	Bundels, Ridgway, Sidbury EX10 0SF
enquiries	T: 01395 597312
EH	House: II

EAST

SY13 91

size	0.6h/1.5a
soil	Clay
altitude	75m/250ft
aspect	Flat, AONB
rainfall	89–102cm/30–35in
temperature	Zone F

Roses should grow around the door of this pretty thatched cottage, and they do. Roses are the dominant feature of the cottage garden – mainly the old varieties grown as bushes, with as many climbers and ramblers as space allows. Since 1985, when the Softlys retired and bought the former farmhouse, dating from the 16th century, they have gardened continuously. Sheltered and secluded, Bundels is an organic garden full of wildlife: the pond is specifically for frogs, newts, and dragonflies; birds and the visiting badgers are encouraged with food. The borders are bursting with old favourites such as bachelor's buttons, herbaceous geraniums, and alchemilla. This is a garden of 'ordered chaos'. Mrs Softly says she is no plantswoman, and many of her favourites came with her, or were given by friends and relatives. Everything is allowed to self-seed, including a giant teasel, which appeared in the middle of a border. A small orchard has been planted with old native apples, such as 'Devonshire Quarrenden' (first grown in 1670); 'Tom Putt' (1790), and 'Pig's Nose Pippin'.

Beyond the garden is woodland, with views to the surrounding countryside. An area of decaying larch trees was cleared to make way for the new planting of native trees, and drifts of spring bulbs are followed by a carpet of wild flowers – a perfect habitat for birds, bats and other wildlife.

55 Bundels

EAST

ST26 00

size	4h/10a
soil	Neutral clay
altitude	120m/400ft
aspect	E-facing slope, AONB
rainfall	76–89cm/30–35in
temperature	Zone F
	Nursery

The ten-acre (4ha) gardens at Burrow Farm have been developed by the Bengers, with visitors in mind. The main garden was planted in 1979, and although it began as a hobby, Mary Benger's plans for a large garden meant that it had to be self-financing. There has been a steady stream of visitors since it opened, with 6,500 people enjoying the gardens in 2002.

A series of different gardens makes excellent use of the site, with its fine views over the Axe valley. The first area to be developed was the courtyard adjoining the house. Here, and throughout, imaginative use of stonework and a variety of hard surfaces gives form and structure to the garden, even in winter. Indeed, many visitors return time and again because, as Mary Benger puts it, there is no one best time of the year. The woodland garden came next: situated in a Roman clay pit, it was the obvious site for a pond and moisture-loving plants. Once the brambles and nettles had been cleared, wild flowers spread themselves unchecked, and the lawns are simply mown field grass. There is also a pergola and a terrace garden, with colour-themed planting schemes to provide interest in the late summer.

To celebrate the millennium, a rill garden was designed, in a position that enjoys full sun. With its central rill, terrace wall and steps, and a delightful summerhouse, it has a Lutyenesque appearance. There are several other areas to be explored, and everywhere the planting is imaginative, with many of the plants stocked in the plant sales area.

56 Burrow Farm Gardens

open	Jul–Aug, Fri + Spring + Aug Bank Holiday, pm
directions	SY08 96, 1ml NW Ottery St Mary on B3176
owner	Mr R. Thistlethwayte
address	Cadhay, Ottery St Mary Admin: Myrtle Place, Gosford Lane, Ottery St Mary EX11 1NA
enquiries	T: 01404 812432
EH	House: I

EAST

SX08 96

size	2.4h/6a
soil	Acid/mixed
altitude	45m/150ft
aspect	Level
rainfall	63–76cm/25–30in
temperature	Zone E

Cadhay takes its name from the de Cadehaye family who held land here in the time of Edward I. In 1527, a de Cadehaye heiress married John Hayden, the builder of the present house, which remained in the family until debts forced its sale in 1736. The next owner remodelled the front, which has remained unaltered since. In the early 19th century, ownership of Cadhay passed to a daughter who decided not to live here, so the house was divided, and let to a tenant farmer. Farm buildings covered the front lawns, and by the time it was sold a century later the house was in a very poor state. The new owner was a Fellow of Trinity College, Cambridge, and it is thanks to his careful restoration that Cadhay survives at all. A major contribution was made by the next owners, the William-Powlett family: the fourth generation of this family now occupies the house.

Work began on the gardens in about 1911, with the removal of the farm buildings. The medieval fish-ponds, linked to the south front by a double row of Irish yews, pre-date the house. The pond surrounds are planted with hostas, primulas, and rodgersias. A gravel walk leads to long herbaceous borders, which were established in the 1930s and are flanked by parallel yew hedges. The borders are rhythmically planted, and contain sufficient shrubs to give form, even when the herbaceous subjects have died back. A ha-ha divides the lawns from the parkland. An impressive avenue of aged lime trees lines the entrance drive, and in spring drifts of daffodils and crocuses bring colour back to gardens which perfectly complement a lovely house.

57 Cadhay

open	Under NGS, May–Jul some Sat, Sun, pm; and May–mid-Aug, Thu pm, and by appt
directions	ST31 06, A358 Axminster to Chard, at Tytherleigh take road to Chardstock, R at George Inn, L fork to Hook, R to Burridge
owners	Mr & Mrs F. Clarkson
address	Dicot, Burridge, Chardstock EX13 7DF
enquiries	T: 01460 220364 www.dicot.co.uk

EAST

ST31 06

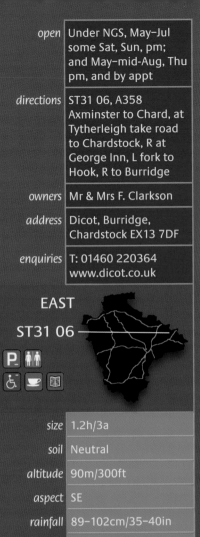

size	1.2h/3a
soil	Neutral
altitude	90m/300ft
aspect	SE
rainfall	89–102cm/35–40in
temperature	Zone E

The gardens here have been developed along the banks of the stream below the Clarksons' cottage. They began in 1986 with the slopes in front of the house, and divided the rest of the three acres (1.2ha) into four separate areas, gradually bringing it all under control. With the help of a mini-digger, the dam of the pond was rebuilt, and many hours were spent clearing out the stream. Unwanted trees and shrubs had to be removed, to make way for more unusual species, and shelterbelts of conifers and hardwoods – including the holly hedge to the north – planted to give protection from the chill winds coming up the valley. The pond – enlarged twice already – has become a focus, and a bog garden is planted with an interesting range of moisture-loving plants, including the bog orchid. Most of the borders, which spread all along the valley, have also had to be extended, to accommodate an ever-increasing collection of plants. The slope below the cottage is filled with numerous azaleas, which create a solid bank of colour in the spring, and there is a variety of small structures to provide interest: a gazebo; a grotto and ruin; a blue shed, and a duck house. The back garden took a whole year to create out of scrub, and is devoted to vegetables. New ideas are always being tried out by the Clarksons: recent developments include a camellia walk and a Japanese garden.

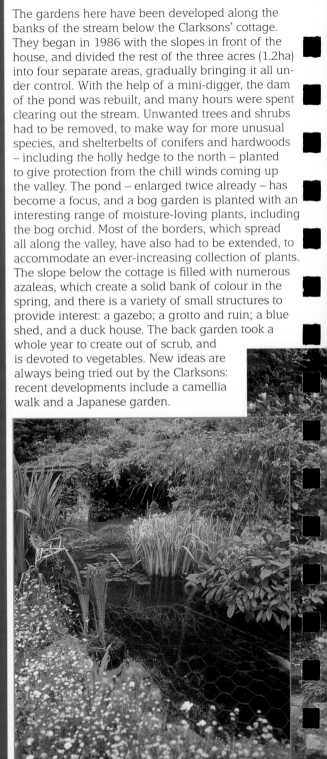

open	Daily, am, pm
directions	SY08 98, A30 Exeter–Honiton, signed at Fairmile
owner	Mr J-M Kennaway
address	Escot, Fairmile, nr Exeter EX11 1LU
enquiries	T: 01404 822188 www.escot-devon.co.uk
EH	House: II

EAST

SY08 98

size	89h/220a, including parkland
soil	Neutral, sandy
altitude	107m/350ft
aspect	Level
rainfall	76–89cm/30–35in
temperature	Zone E
	Plant sales

Set in 220 acres (89ha) of parkland laid out by Sir Walter Yonge, the present house at Escot was built in 1808 for John Kennaway, after fire destroyed the original building. The Kennaway family still lives here. Behind the house are some magnificent specimen trees, many of them listed, a few of which survive from the original planting. Of particular note are the vast *Wellingtonia*, a huge London plane tree, and a recumbent Lucombe oak. This garden is a treat for those who love trees.

There is plenty to interest visitors of all ages at Escot. The woodlands – planted with azaleas and rhododendrons – courtyard, and kitchen garden are now home to a variety of birds and mammals – including birds of prey, otters, wild boar, and red squirrels – and there are adventure playgrounds for children to explore. There are also ice-ponds and an ice-house, and a collection of exotic plants. Ivan Hicks has revived the immediate gardens and shrubbery, and further restoration work is planned. Entry to the wildfowl and wetland areas by the ponds is free. Escot has a growing reputation as an educational centre, and is popular with many primary schools and centres for people with disabilities. In the summer, falconry displays take place frequently. The former stables house a restaurant, shop, and craft centre.

59 Escot Fantasy Garden

open	Under NGS. Nursery: Mar–Jul, Aug–Oct, am, pm, and by appt
directions	SY01 99, B3181 Exeter–Taunton at Dog village to Whimple, fork L to Westwood
owners	Mr & Mrs M. Squires
address	1 Feebers Cottage, Westwood, nr Broadclyst, EX5 3DQ
enquiries	T: 01404 822118

EAST

SY01 99

size	0.4h/1a
soil	Heavy clay
altitude	46m/150ft
aspect	Level
rainfall	76–89cm/30–35in
temperature	Zone F
	Nursery

The cottage is part of the **Killerton** (42) estate, and is thought to have been the original dame school for the hamlet. Between it and the listed outbuilding, which could have been the privy, is an underlying area of clinker – the playground perhaps?

The small garden feels much larger than it is. When the Squires moved into the cottage in the 1970s, they could see no trace of a garden until some blackcurrant bushes came to light when they began clearing. These bushes are still bearing fruit today. The trees that they planted in their initial enthusiasm have matured to provide a perfect habitat for shade-loving plants, which flourish here. Planting schemes have been designed to cope with occasional flooding, late frosts, and stodgy clay. Some gardeners would consider gardening in these conditions an impossibility; but the Squires have installed new drainage channels to reduce the risk of flooding, and learned how to make the best of the clay: Mrs Squires now produces a leaflet in which she gives valuable advice to other gardeners struggling with similar soil types. She is highly successful in propagating speciality plants, many of which are for sale, in the four greenhouses. An organizer for the NCCPG, she is also on the *RHS Plant Finder* list.

Wildlife is encouraged in this organic garden. Plenty of seats are surrounded with changing displays of plants in pots, and the vegetable patch is as attractive as the rest of the garden. Raised beds contain a collection of alpine plants.

60 1 Feebers Cottage

open	Under NGS, and by appt
directions	(J) SY16 89, 2ml NE of Sidmouth on A3052. Use NT car-park in Weston (T) SY15 89, on A 3052 nr donkey sanctuary
owners	(J) Mrs S.A. Macfadyen (T) Mr J. Langston & Mr M. Burgess
address	Jasmine Cottage, Weston, nr Sidmouth EX10 0PH Turnpike Cottage, Salcombe Regis, Sidmouth EX10 0PB
enquiries	T: (J) 01395 512238 T: (T) 01395 515265
EH	House: (J) II

EAST

(J) SY16 89
(T) SY15 89

P   ♿

🚻 ☕ 🐕

size	(J) 0.4h/1a (T) 0.3h/0.75a
soil	(J) Neutral loam (T) Clay, chalky lumps
altitude	(J) 160m/525ft (T) 156m/515ft
aspect	Level, AONB
rainfall	76–89cm/30–35in
temperature	Zone F
	(T) Plant sales + seed nursery

The organic garden at **Jasmine Cottage** (top right and below) is a haven for wild birds: emphasis is placed on gardening with nature, and Mrs Macfadyen encourages over 30 species of bird to visit by scattering seeds for them throughout the garden. Cruel winds are a problem, despite the sheltering walls that surround the garden, so plants begin their life in pots to see if they can survive before being planted out permanently. Surrounding the thatched cottage, which is nearly 400 years old, is a pretty, informal garden, which develops as and when Mrs Macfadyen comes across a plant that catches her eye, and which she feels would fit in well. The effect is delightful, and the garden has a number of different areas, from wild corners to a paved Mediterranean area by the kitchen door, and soft grasses by the front door.

As a combined opening with Jasmine Cottage, the narrow strip of garden at **Turnpike Cottage** (below right) is very different. The owners run their own seed company, and the garden is something of a trial ground, with plants required to set seed before being cut back. They are enthusiastic plantsmen, returning from holidays laden with seed that will ultimately find its way into their catalogue, or on to their stand at the RHS Chelsea Flower Show. Although the plot is long and narrow, the garden is full of exuberant planting, and can boast both wet and dry areas, and a woodland, as well as the borders. It is estimated that there are about 1,500 different species growing here, and although full of interest all through the year, the garden is particularly lovely in the spring.

61 Jasmine Cottage
& Turnpike Cottage

open	Under NGS, one Sat, Sun each Jul, Aug, pm, and by appt
directions	SY10 97, 10ml from M5. Leave new A30 at Iron Bridge from Honiton, Pattersons X from Exeter on old A30
owners	Mr & Mrs R. Reid
address	Little Ash Farm, Fennybridges, Honiton EX14 3BL
enquiries	T: 01404 850271

EAST

SY10 97

P P

size	0.3h/0.75a
soil	Sandy
altitude	45m/150ft
aspect	SE
rainfall	76–89cm/30–35in
temperature	Zone E

This garden seems designed for relaxation, with many shady arbours and plenty of seats. By careful planning, a garden of great variety has been achieved on what was a bare site with just one pear tree. Bob Reid, who is a furniture-maker, has constructed paths and timber steps; delightful stone walls, and two ponds fed from a basin from which the water overflows into a narrow, stone-lined rill. The sound used to help drown the noise of traffic, but since the construction of a new road to the north, which has restored peace to Little Ash Farm, the water attracts plenty of wildlife.

The garden is beautifully maintained, and its strength is a good basic design that remains attractive whatever the season. Sadie Reid grows only what does well: plants are used repeatedly and to great effect, with cool shady borders, and bright sunny areas. Trelliswork and a pergola are covered with climbers, and trees have been planted carefully to enhance the space. Raised vegetable beds and an area of soft fruit provide an abundance of home-grown produce. This garden is full of clever ideas – not least, how to construct a nine-hole golf-course on just three lawns. Bob Reid's workshop and show-room are generally open to visitors.

open	Under NGS, Apr–May, some Sun, Mon, am, pm, and by appt
directions	SY32 94, A3070 Lyme Regis–Axminster, R to Rocombe, 0.25ml, park on verge by field gate
owner	Mrs E. Marriage
address	The Moorings, Rocombe, Lyme Regis DT7 3RR
enquiries	T: 01297 443295

EAST

SY32 94

size	1.2h/3a
soil	Stony sand, some clay
altitude	75–120m/250–400ft
aspect	W + S, steep, AONB
rainfall	76–89cm/30–35in
temperature	Zone E

Many years of hard work by Enid Marriage and her late husband have gone into the creation of this woodland garden. When they moved to The Moorings in 1965, the Marriages took possession of three fields of gorse, brambles, and scrub, situated on a steeply sloping hillside – not the most propitious of sites on which to develop a garden. A bulldozer was brought in to level a series of zigzag paths from top to bottom of the slope, after which the first trees were planted by Mr Marriage. There are glades of silver birch and hollies; native trees are mixed with species of foreign origin – tall stands of eucalyptus were grown from seed sent from Australia, and are now a major feature. At the very bottom of the garden, next to the house, is a magnificent *Eucryphia*. Here is the only level area in the garden, with a small lawn and rockery-style planting, with banks of primroses, grape hyacinths and cistus in spring. Helped by the Marriages over the years, snowdrops have naturalized beneath the trees, and provide an almost continuous carpet of flowers, followed by bluebells and periwinkle. Wild flowers have also colonized the woodland. These days, the only maintenance required is the occasional felling of a tree, and pruning back of the shrubs. The garden first opened under the NGS scheme in 1986, and is at its best in spring and autumn.

63 The Moorings

open	Under NGS, Jun, some pm
directions	SX99 84, in village, after church R up Burgmanns Hill, R into Manor House car-park
owners	Mr & Mrs J.W. Pankhurst
address	The Old Garden, Burgmanns Hill, Lympstone, Exmouth EX8 5HP
enquiries	T: 01395 272010

EAST

SX99 84

size	0.1h/0.33a
soil	Alkaline, rich
altitude	30m/100ft
aspect	E/W
rainfall	76–89cm/30–35in
temperature	Zone E
	Plant sales

'The Secret Garden' would have been just as appropriate a name for this property, as the bungalow and garden are out of sight, reached via the entrance to the Manor House. When the Manor was divided into flats, the garden area behind was sold off to the Pankhursts, divided from its neighbour by high, old redbrick walls. The new owners hacked their way to the far end of the plot to find out what they had bought, and discovered a venerable old Bramley, at least 150 years old, which still bears fruit. Mrs Pankhurst remembers a complete absence of worms, and soil that set like concrete. For three years they grew potatoes, then built their home, before beginning work on the garden – now home to plenty of worms. Mrs Pankhurst describes the result of that work as a 'miniature large garden' – a phrase that captures well the many varied elements of the area. To the front is a bed of grasses and alpines, while at the rear neatly trimmed hedges define the different areas, one of the oldest being the ericaceous border of rhododendrons, azaleas, and ericas. Trees, including a walnut, were planted early on, in the late 1960s and now provide shade and structure in the garden. Some shrubs and trees are kept clipped into mushroom shapes, giving an air of quiet formality and control. It is difficult to believe that Mrs Pankhurst never sat down to plan the garden: she says it just grew, but to achieve so much in a restricted space requires thought and skill.

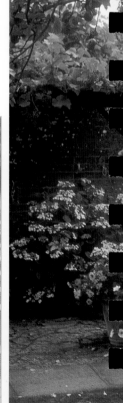

64 The Old Garden

open	Under NGS, one Sat, Sun Jul, and by appt
directions	SY24 92, W end of Colyford, turn off A3052 into lane, go past Colyton Grammar School, walk up lane
owners	Mr & Mrs A. Davis
address	Paddocks, Stafford Lane, Colyford EX24 6HQ
enquiries	T: 01297 552472

EAST

SY24 92

size	0.8h/2a
soil	Stony clay with sand
altitude	45m/150ft
aspect	SSE, AONB
rainfall	76–89cm/30–35in
temperature	Zone F
	Plant sales

Island beds were just coming into fashion when the gardens were originally laid out around this 1950s bungalow. It sits two-thirds of the way up a spacious, gently sloping lawn, with views across the valley towards the sea. Conifers, and beds of winter-flowering heathers were also in vogue, both of which are to be found here. The Davises resisted the temptation to sweep away everything and redesign the garden when they moved here in 1996: the large beds were well planned, and the shrubs mature, so they remain a feature. Instead, they turned their attentions to the areas closer to the bungalow. Change has been gradual, but the owners feel that the garden is now more satisfactory, and owes as much to them as to previous owners. Wendy Davis grows a wide variety of flowers for cutting and arranging, and has introduced some colourful borders for this purpose. She is also good at planting containers, which are grouped on the terraces to give a display throughout the season. At the top of the garden is the large and productive vegetable garden – Alan Davis' province. He has introduced several new areas, including a bog garden, a wild-flower patch, and a belt of specimen trees, partly aimed at breaking the wind that cuts across the valley.

EAST

SY23 89

P P₊ ♿ ♟

🍴 📖 🛍 ⛩

size	4.4h/11a
soil	Sandy/chalky
altitude	30m/100ft
aspect	S slope, AGLV
rainfall	76–89cm/30–35in
temperature	Zone E

High above the fishing village of Beer is the world of Pecorama, a major tourist attraction with unexpectedly good gardens. Such places usually content themselves with basic bedding schemes and a few fuchsias, interspersed between the main attractions. At Pecorama, the attraction is a miniature railway, with little steam trains running around the 11-acre (4.4ha) site. The railway was installed on the chalk hillside in 1974, when the business that manufactures and sells model trains and their accessories moved here. A large quantity of topsoil – much of it from the Seaton Tennis Club, which was constructing hard courts to replace grass at that time – was imported to improve the chalky soil.

Gardeners do not expect the treat in store for them when they climb up the hill past the waiting trains. The transformation of the former Pitch-and-Put course began in 1998, and is the vision of Michael Pritchard, son of the founder, Sidney. The Secret Garden had already been completed, and with the help of designer Naila Green the Millennium gardens were laid out. The concept was a series of themed gardens to take advantage of the sloping site: they can be viewed from above, and are linked by wandering paths, with higher walkways and a viewing platform over the Chelsea-style displays. The nearest thing to a bedding scheme is the Rainbow Garden and, yes, it is parsley that forms the green band. Four gardeners maintain the whole site, which includes woodlands and a wildlife area.

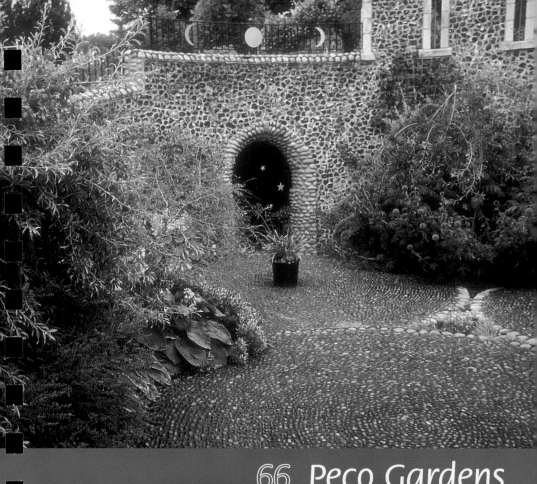

66 Peco Gardens

open	Under NGS, one Sat, Sun, May, pm, and as advertised
directions	SY20 93, from A375 Honiton–Sidmouth, follow signs to Southleigh. Park by village hall
owners	(P): Mr & Mrs E. Daniels (M): Mr & Mrs Tarling
address	Pope's Cottage, Southleigh, Colyton EX24 6SB Mulberry House, Southleigh, Colyton EX24 6SB
enquiries	T: (P) 01404 871210; (M) 01404 871566

EAST
SY20 93

size	(P) 0.3ha/0.66a (M) 0.4ha/1a
soil	Lime-free
altitude	80m/263ft
aspect	South-facing
rainfall	50cm/20in
temperature	Zone E

In the tucked-away hamlet of Southleigh, a stream runs past the bottom of the garden of **Pope's Cottage** (top right). The Daniels have gardened here since 1990, using the framework of existing trees, which include several magnolias and some fine silver birches. Several conifers have been removed, and new trees carefully sited to preserve the views across the valley. The little erigeron daisy runs riot around the terrace, where tender climbers cling to the walls, and delicate subjects are grown in pots. A scree slope leads down to the lawns, which are divided by beds of rhododendrons and other ericaceous plants on soil kept acid by the stream that feeds ponds at the lower end. Cottage favourites including lupins, irises and delphiniums grow in beds along the higher boundary, jumbled up with roses and fruit bushes. Paths meander between the beds, and under clematis- and rose-covered arches.

The garden at **Mulberry House** (below and bottom right) dates from 1998, when the Tarlings moved here. Thomasina Tarling is a knowledgeable gardener, and she has divided the sloping acre (0.4 ha) into separate compartments, each with its own character and colour theme. The garden has been planned so that there is something of interest throughout the year. Drifts of grasses and a backbone of shrubs and trees, including cherries, conifers, silver birches, *Acers* and *Cornus* provide winter form. Purple and cream are the colour theme of one long border, with *Berberis*, *Photinia*, *Philadelphus* and a red *Robinia*, *Phormiums* and purple hazel. Hollyhocks, almost black in colour, are raised annually from seed, as are white cosmos. Creamy white plantings surround a magnolia, and throughout preference is given to good foliage and shape. A stream has been diverted to a pond before cascading down beside the house. Clematis scramble over trellises, with cistus, helianthemums and perennial stocks in any corner where there is space.

67 Southleigh Gardens

open	Under NGS, some Sat, Sun, Jun, pm
directions	SY27 98, from Axminster on A35 L before Old Inn (to Whitford), park village hall car-park, 200yd on R next village store
owners	Mr & Mrs A.J. Lucas
address	Ways Cottage, Kilmington, Axminster EX13 7RG
enquiries	T: 01297 33279
EH	House: II

EAST

SY27 98

size	0.2h/0.33h
soil	Loam, slightly alkaline
altitude	60m/200ft
aspect	SSW
rainfall	76–89cm/30–35in
temperature	Zone D

If trees and large shrubs had been planted here, they would have dominated the garden behind this cottage, which dates from the 1650s and is tucked away just off the village street. The few that have been permitted are therefore confined to the outer edges, and the owners are thankful that the perimeter planting has grown sufficiently over the years to blot out new development, which was permitted to within a few feet of their boundary. Because of the alkaline soil, the emphasis is on herbaceous perennials, roses and plants with good shape and form, including *Eryngiums*, *Phlomis*, *Campanula*, and grasses. Although the Lucases have done plenty to the cottage, which was originally two, the garden had to wait until the children no longer needed room to kick a ball around. But they have more than made up for lost time, and they have explored the potential of a small area to the full. The changes in level have been well planned, and several intimate corners are incorporated into the design without creating a feeling of claustrophobia. The small pond is home to a thriving population of frogs.

Jane Lucas is a keen garden visitor, and generally returns home with plenty of ideas, and plenty of plants. There is a friendly and welcoming feel to this garden, and you will leave with a host of tips.

68 Ways Cottage

open	Under NGS, some Sat, Sun, Mar–Sep, am, pm, and by appt
directions	SY08 09, B3178 Newton Poppleford–Colaton Raleigh L (to Dotton) immediately R, 0.25ml, 1st house on R
owners	Mrs M. Herbert, Mrs McKay & Mr E. Stevenson
address	Yonder Hill, Shepherds Lane, Colaton Raleigh EX10 0LP
enquiries	T: 01395 567541

EAST

SY08 09

size	1.00h/2.5a
soil	Acid, sandy, pH4–5.5
altitude	60m/220ft
aspect	N slope, AONB
rainfall	63–76cm/25–30in
temperature	Zone E
	Plant sales

Designed by Eddie Stevenson, the garden at Yonder Hill was begun in 1992 for Mollie Herbert, by her daughter, Judy. The first plantings were confined to the area around the bungalow – originally a beach café at Exmouth – but now extend to cover the whole site. There are plans to create new woodland areas as well. The trees and shrubs thrive in the mild east Devon climate, and produce a phenomenal rate of growth. The Herberts used to run a nursery, and the planting schemes have been thoughtfully designed to provide year-round interest: many of the beds contain three flushes of plants, which combine to produce a long display. There are large numbers of trees here, especially birches and aspens, and Judy's great passions, eucalyptus and pine – about 30 different varieties of each. Grasses and willows are grown throughout the garden.

The paths around the lower garden are somewhat like a maze, but it is delightful to be lost in such surroundings. An unusual feature is the 'letter beds', which are laid out in the shape of the family's initials, and planted with favourites, including 'E' (Eddie): conifers and heathers; 'J' (Judy): bamboo and eucalyptus, and 'M' (Mollie): hostas and alstromeria – a highly original variation on the idea of planting a commemorative tree. Wildlife abounds; exotic birds are plentiful, and a small herd of goats lives off the prunings and clippings in the adjoining field.

69 Yonder Hill

Lying to the south of the busy main road between Exeter and Plymouth, this part of Devon is a landscape of deep combes and wooded hillsides. Beautiful rivers – the Erme, Yealm, Avon, and Dart – drain off the heights of Dartmoor, ending in deep, tidal creeks, separated from each other by high, windswept cliffs. The heights of Start Point and Bolt Head on the coast have wonderful views, and the Eddystone lighthouse can be seen from the latter. Historically, this was not a prosperous area: there was no mining or manufacturing, just a number of small seafaring communities along the coast, and farms inland. This began to change with the coming of the railway, and today the waters are crowded with sleek yachts and opulent cruisers.

Between the estuaries of the Plym and the Dart are the South Hams: the name is taken from the Old English word *hamme*, meaning a sheltered place, and subtropical plants thrive here. Several of the beautiful coastal gardens – **Blackpool Gardens** (70) and **Coleton Fishacre** (73), for example – have unexpectedly large examples of shrubs and trees that would struggle to survive inland.

Totnes, dominated by the castle, is an ancient Saxon burgh on the bank of the Dart. Wool and the cloth trade were its greatest source of wealth, which continued until the end of the 17th century. Dartmouth has one of the oldest deep-water harbours in the country. From here both the Second and Third Crusades set sail in the 12th century, and Drake used Dartmouth as his home port when he saw off the Spanish Armada in 1588. Raleigh and Gilbert also had roots in the area, and knew the waters well. Dartmouth continued to prosper in medieval times, being an important port for the Normans trading across the Channel with France, and through it much of the cloth from the south Devon textile industry was exported. When this trade died out, new markets across the Atlantic were opened up, and the fish trade with Newfoundland

brought prosperity to the little port. But poor communications with the rest of the country, and the increasing size of shipping, caused decline. The naval college was built in 1905, replacing a succession of training ships moored in the estuary.

Newton Abbot and Torquay are served by Brunel's Great Western Railway, and

5 SOUTH

were deliberately developed to take advantage of the growing holiday boom. Torquay was originally a small fishing village, and looks out over a beautiful bay, which suddenly found itself providing a base for the fleet at the time of the Napoleonic wars. (Napoleon himself was held in a ship moored in the bay for almost two months, after his defeat at Waterloo.)

At this time, the Continent was closed to English visitors, and naval families began visiting Torbay, the 'English Riviera'. After the extension of the line from Newton Abbot, the railway reached Torquay in 1848, and the town became a prosperous Victorian resort with well-planned terraces and squares, and a promenade planted with the now-famous palm trees.

open	Apr–Oct, daily, am, pm
directions	SX85 47, follow Blackpool Sands signs from Dartmouth for 3ml on A379. Between Stoke Fleming and Strete. Entry through Blackpool Sands car-park
owner	Sir Geoffrey Newman
address	Blackpool Sands, Dartmouth TQ6 0RG
enquiries	T: 01803 770606 E: info@ blackpoolsands.co.uk www.blackpoolsands. co.uk

SOUTH
SX85 47

size	1.2h/3a
soil	Lime-free loam
altitude	15–30m/50–100ft
aspect	S-sloping, AONB, Heritage Coast
rainfall	102–127cm/40–50in
temperature	Zone H

Blackpool was the childhood home of the present owner, Sir Geoffrey Newman, and the gardens the areas in which he used to play. Only recently has the significance of these gardens been realized, and work undertaken to uncover a large collection of rare trees and shrubs, most of them natives of the Southern hemisphere. Thanks to the meticulous records and photographs kept by his grandfather, Robert Newman, and later by his father, Sir Ralph, there is a comprehensive catalogue of the species planted here over the years. Blackpool had originally been a holiday home, where Sir Geoffrey's grandfather could relax from his busy life as Deputy Governor of the Bank of England. Robert Newman quickly entered into the fashion for planting new-found species such as *Acacia*, *Erythrina*, *Eucryphia*, *Feijoa*, *Callistemon*, and *Magnolia*, and in the mild climate of south Devon they flourished. The Newman family's association with the port wine trade resulted in a fine collection of cork oaks, planted in 1896.

A long period of neglect set in following the death of Sir Ralph in 1968, and it was not until Sir Geoffrey moved back in the 1980s that the potential of the gardens was realized. With European funding, he set about preparing the gardens for opening to the public, reconstructing paths and steps, and clearing undergrowth. Some of the rarities began to emerge, and were accurately identified. Newly cleared areas have been replanted, keeping to the spirit of the original garden, with plants from the Southern hemisphere. The next phase is to clear the upper garden, centred around a small pond, and re-create the wonder of this elevated position with its stunning sea views and distant headlands seen through a canopy of trees and shrubs.

70 Blackpool Gardens

open	See local posters
directions	SX74 38, turn down opposite church in village, park below church
owners	Miss I. Waterhouse & Miss A. Parish
address	Churchpark Cottage, East Portlemouth, Salcombe TQ8 8PF
enquiries	T: 01548 8435572
EH	House: II

SOUTH

SX74 38

size	0.4h/1a
soil	Mixture – neutral
altitude	100m/320ft
aspect	NE, steep slope, AONB
rainfall	89–102cm/35–40in
temperature	Zone A
	Plant sales

Creating a garden on such an exposed site as this was never going to be easy. Above the cottage – parts of which date from the 16th century – the land rises to a plateau, surrounded on three sides by the Salcombe Estuary. It was originally windswept and bare of anything except brambles and blackthorn. Gradually, protection has grown up, but the cold northerlies can cause havoc. Ms Waterhouse and Ms Parish are keen travellers, and have brought back many cuttings and seeds of tender plants from the Antipodes and South Africa. The mild climate of the south coast suits such plants, and at Churchpark Cottage many varieties of *Callistemon*, *Leptospermum*, *Grevillea*, and *Acacia* look very much at home. There is also a good collection of *Hebes*.

The garden spreads up the hillside, and is full of surprises. It is divided into nine different areas, with hedges giving all-important shelter. Over the years as one compartment was finished, so a new area was begun, each with a different feel. Everything is closely planted; wild flowers and wildlife are encouraged. One of the best views is from the orchard, out over the estuary and across to Dartmoor.

71 Churchpark Cottage

open	Daily, am, pm
directions	SX89 63, 1ml Torquay seafront, follow signs to Cockington village
owner	Torbay Coast & Countryside Trust
address	Cockington Court, Torquay TQ2 6XA
enquiries	T: 01803 606035 E: info@countryside-trust.org.uk www.countryside-trust.org.uk
EH	House: II

SOUTH

SX89 63

size	180h/450a parkland
soil	Lime-free
altitude	75m/250ft
aspect	SE, AGLV
rainfall	89–102cm/35–40in
temperature	Zone C
NC	*Carya*

The de Cockington family came over with William the Conqueror, and took possession of the manor where they remained until 1350. Only two other families owned the estate until the late 1930s when the Cockington Trust was formed to preserve 'unchanged the ancient amenities and character' of the estate, and it was handed over to Torbay Council. The present manor house dates from Tudor times, but was extensively remodelled in 1673.

The grounds were largely laid out in the latter part of the 19th century by Richard Mallock. They are beautifully maintained and contain many fine specimen trees, including the National Collection of *Carya* (hickory) trees. The series of lakes at the lower end of the valley are much older, and were originally the fishponds for the house. Today they are surrounded by banks of rhododendrons and camellias, and are home to a population of well-fed ducks. Behind

the Court, a rose garden has been planted on the site of the former menagerie, and there is a demonstration kitchen garden that aims to illustrate organic and sustainable methods of gardening.

Cockington village is a great tourist attraction, with its picturesque cob and thatch cottages and narrow lanes. A new model village was planned by the Cockington Trust, and plans were drawn up by Sir Edwin Lutyens. But all that was built was the distinctive Drum Inn, with its recently restored Lutyens-designed gardens.

open	Mar: Sat, Sun; Apr–Oct: Wed–Sun; Bank Holiday Mon; am, pm
directions	SX90 50, from A379 Torbay–Dartmouth follow tourist signs
owner	NT
address	Coleton Fishacre, Kingswear, Dartmouth TQ6 0EQ
enquiries	T: 01803 752466 E: coletonfishacre@ nationaltrust.org.uk www.nationaltrust. org.uk
EH	House: II

SOUTH

SX90 50

EH	Gardens: II*
size	9.7ha/24a
soil	Acid/silty clay
altitude	30–100m/100–325ft
aspect	W, AONB
rainfall	89–102cm/35–40in
temperature	Zone C
	Plant sales

There is a Cornish feel to this lush, 24-acre (9.7ha) garden of exotic plants, set in a valley leading down to the sea. The house was designed by Oswald Milne after the style of Lutyens, his mentor, and built in 1925 for Rupert D'Oyly Carte. At that time shelter-belts, including pine and holm oak, were planted on either side of the site. The garden itself – one of the last to be constructed in the short-lived era of peace and prosperity between the two World Wars – was designed with much stone terracing and paving, semicircular steps, and pools. The central stream is confined to a rill running through a formal walled garden close to the house, from which it escapes to cascade down to the beach, through groves of bamboos, hydrangeas, and many tender and subtropical plants. The broad terrace in front of the house was intended as a platform from which to view the sea, but the trees have now grown up to obscure this. When the National Trust became the custodian of Coleton Fishacre in 1983, the garden had been maintained, but there was a great deal of clearing and thinning to be undertaken. Taking the visitor through glades and groves, paths traversing the valley lead to the coastal path, and the cove where the D'Oyly Cartes once had a bathing-pool and a landing-stage for their yacht (now inaccessible). There are wonderful views of the sea from the gazebo.

open	Under NGS, am, pm. Phone for details
directions	SX86 70, A380 Newton Abbott, at Penn roundabout follow signs town centre; 1st L, 1st R, 2nd L
owners	Betty & Don Frampton
address	Collepardo, 3 Keyberry Park, Newton Abbott TQ12 1DF
enquiries	T: 01626 354580

SOUTH

SX86 70

size	0.13ha/0.33a
soil	Neutral stony
altitude	30m/100ft
aspect	S
rainfall	102–114cm/40–45in
temperature	Zone D
	Plant sales

About 1,500 plants came with Don and Betty Frampton when they moved here in 1994, to transform a garden that consisted largely of grass, a 7m *Cupressus leylandii* hedge, and some trees. Betty and Don worked on the design together, keeping the terrace, but laying out new paths and beds. All the grass went; the hedge is down to a manageable height, and everywhere there are now specimen trees, shrubs, herbaceous perennials, and alpines. A series of separate areas is defined by trelliswork or taller shrubs, and linked by gravel paths. Arches connect, hosting a variety of climbers to draw the eye upwards. More climbers cover the gazebo, which is made from recycled timber, and from which there is a good view over the garden. In this densely planted garden, a programme of rigorous pruning keeps potential giants, such as roses 'Paul's Himalayan Musk' and 'Kiftsgate', within bounds. Betty does not suffer from timidity in her planting schemes: many unusual plants flourish among a variety of old favourites. This relatively small garden contains a surprising variety of environments, from hot, dry beds, to the damp soil around the pond, where the sound of water trickling down a brick column is a pleasant feature.

74 Collepardo

open	Daily, am, pm
directions	SX79 62, off A384 Buckfastleigh–Totnes, L at parish church
owner	Dartington Hall Trust
address	Dartington Hall, Totnes TQ9 6EL
enquiries	T: 01803 862367 E: gardens@ dartingtonhall.org.uk
EH	House: I

SOUTH

SX79 62

EH	Gardens: II*
size	4h/10a
soil	Acid
altitude	46–61m/150–200ft
aspect	S, AGLV
rainfall	114–127cm/45–50in
temperature	Zone E
	Plant sales

The whole of this remarkable site is steeped in history, going back to the 1380s when the medieval hall was built for John Holland – the half brother of Richard II – and his wife, a daughter of John of Gaunt. Other owners have included the Earl of Devon, and the Champernowne family. The estate was purchased in 1925 by Leonard and Dorothy Elmhirst, with the intention of running Dartington as a centre for rural skills. Their idea was successful, and the medieval buildings are at the heart of a campus dedicated to the arts and rural concerns. Since the deaths of the Elmhirsts, Dartington Hall has been run by a Trust: Dorothy Elmhirst's wish that Dartington be a 'place of experiment' is kept alive.

The Elmhirsts had sufficient wealth to restore not only the beautiful old buildings, but the grounds as well. The jousting green is believed to date from the earliest days, and it is here that many of the oldest trees are located, as well as the 12 topped yews known as The Apostles. The foremost garden designers were called in: Avray Tipping, Beatrix Farrand, and Percy Cane all had a hand. Each tree and shrub was carefully chosen and sited, with modern sculpture adding a further dimension. Dartington is about space and tranquillity, about form and shape, and the relationship of one area with another, rather than being a garden of botanical rarities. There is colour throughout the year, starting with carpets of crocus and daffodils, and magnificent evergreen magnolias growing against the old stone walls, which also provide a frame for many wall shrubs and fine climbers. There are glades of azaleas and rhododendrons, hydrangeas and shrubs for autumn colour, and throughout, many wonderful trees.

75 Dartington Hall Gardens

open	Mar–Jul, Sun, Bank Holiday Mon, am, pm, and by appt
directions	SX83 49, 1.5 ml W Dartmouth off A3122 Totnes road, L at signpost to Hillfield
owners	Mr & Mrs A.S. Mort
address	Fast Rabbit Farm, Ash Cross, Dartmouth TQ6 OLR
enquiries	T: 01803 712437 E: fastrabbitfarm@ beeb.net www.fastrabbitfarm. co.uk

SOUTH
SX83 49

size	6h/13a
soil	Slightly acid
altitude	145m/450ft
aspect	SSW, AGLV
rainfall	114–127cm/48–50in
temperature	Zone D
	Nursery

The unusual name was coined by the children of the family, soon after they began their business in 1990. The farm was and is host to a number of wild hares. An old collie – an enthusiastic ratter – was new to the concept of hares. They were explained as 'fast rabbits', creating excitement and a futile chase. What began as a nursery with a small landscaping business attached has changed around, with the nursery feeding the design business. The farm is run as part of the Countryside Stewardship Scheme, and the area is a wildlife haven. The farm consists of 146 acres (59ha), with 13 acres (5ha) of gardens in the valley, and 30 acres (12ha) of woodland. The farmhouse and nursery are at the highest point, and while separated from the garden, future plans for a visitor centre, new car-park, and farm track will link all features. Over the years the Morts have planted trees and shrubs, and the gardens are a surprising mix of ornamental planting juxtaposed with wild flowers and native trees. There are many camellias, magnolias, and rhododendrons, as well as a rockery area. Water has been exploited, with small ponds created wherever they found a spring, all feeding the main stream, the River Black, which meanders through the gardens. Birds are everywhere, and in spring the bluebells draw hundreds of visitors.

The nursery tunnels are well stocked with a wide variety of plants, most home-propagated. The next phase is an educational centre, where Stevie and Alan Mort plan to run courses in wildlife conservation.

76　Fast Rabbit Farm

open	Mar–Oct, Wed–Sat, am, pm. House not open
directions	SX87 65, follow signs for Greenway Quay and Ferry from A379 Torbay–Brixham. Parking only if pre-booked. Greenways to Greenway ferry from Dartmouth, T: 01803 834488.
owner	NT
address	Greenway, Greenway Road, Galmpton, Churston Ferrers TQ5 0ES
enquiries	T: 01803 842382 E: greenway@ nationaltrust.org.uk www.nationaltrust. org.uk
EH	House: II*

SOUTH

SX87 65

size	13h/30a
soil	Acid, shale
altitude	100m/320ft
aspect	W + S, AONB
rainfall	89–102cm/35–40in
temperature	Zone C
	Plant sales

Few gardens can claim to have been constructed by a labour force of 160 Spanish prisoners of war. Situated on the banks of the River Dart, just above Dartmouth, it is not surprising that the house has been owned by a succession of well-known seafaring families, and it was Sir John Gilbert who put his Armada prisoners to work in the grounds. The present house was built in 1790, and some trees from that time survive in the woodland. By the mid-19th century the garden had been laid out much as it is today, with the camellia garden, walled garden, and riverside walks. There is also a fernery, a vinery, and a peach house. More camellias, rhododendrons, magnolias, and spring bulbs were added in the early 20th century by Thomas Bolitho and his son-in-law Charles Williams, who owned the garden from 1880 to 1932. In 1938, Greenway became the holiday home of Agatha Christie. Her daughter and son-in-law, Mr and Mrs A. Hicks, have added plantings of their own, particularly species from the Southern hemisphere. There is an atmosphere of timelessness and tranquility, which are experienced by the visitor wandering through the woodland and catching glimpses of the Dart. Down at the water's edge is a rare survivor, a 19th-century bath-house whose 2m-deep plunge-pool is filled by the river at high tide.

Given to the National Trust in 2000, the estate is now subject to a ten-year plan of restoration and consolidation. The newly restored camellia garden opened in 2003, and there are plans for the restoration of the vinery over the next few years.

open	Under NGS, May Bank Holiday Sun, Mon, and by appt, am, pm
directions	SX86 54, from Red Lion follow The Level to fork, go straight up steep lane to River Farm gate and follow signs
owners	Mr & Mrs R. McCrum
address	Hamblyn's Coombe, Dittisham, Dartmouth TQ6 0HE
enquiries	T: 01803 722228

SOUTH

SX86 54

size	2.8h/7a
soil	Mildly acid; part rock
altitude	30–100m/100–325ft
aspect	ENE, AONB
rainfall	89–102cm/35–40in
temperature	Zone C
	Plant sales

The magic of the Dart Estuary drew the McCrums to their out-of-the-way cottage in 1984. The steep slope, covered in primroses and bluebells, and reaching to the water's edge, clinched the deal, and they found themselves the owners of what was originally a woodsman's cottage, built in 1837. Apart from the dramatic setting, the seven-acre (2.8ha) garden is noteworthy on two counts: Bridget McCrum is a sculptor of international renown, using the garden as a showcase; and Robert McCrum is a keen and knowedgeable gardener who has made good use of the site. The McCrums planned the layout together, and everywhere there are sculptures of birds and animals. On a level with the house is a well-planned formal garden with clipped shrubs and hedges, against which several sculptures are displayed; a modern fountain, and a pretty pond. This leads to a one-person meditation court surrounded by clipped yew.

Recently added to the house is the painting studio, which won a RIBA award; the gallery narrowly missed the same accolade earlier. With a backdrop of woodland and a mildly acid soil, rhododendrons, camellias and azaleas do well, and Robert McCrum's philosophy is to plant in blocks of colour rather than mix everything up. As one area fades, another comes into flower, so that interest is continued throughout the year. Masses of hydrangeas line the stream, with late colour provided by the fuchsias, parrotias, liquidambers and nyssa. Throughout there are bamboos and ferns flourishing in the moist air, and higher up acers have established themselves well.

SOUTH

SX81 65

size	0.3h/0.75a
soil	Lime, pH 6.5–6.9
altitude	30m/100ft
aspect	S + E
rainfall	89–102cm/35–40in
temperature	Zone F
	Plant sales

The first trees were planted on this valley site in 1990, but at that time the owners were farming across the road, and their plan was to convert the hay barn into a couple of holiday cottages, which they did very successfully. The garden would have to wait until later, and is still in its early stages, the Holls having moved into the barn only in 1995. Ann Holl started gardening at the top of the slope, and is working her way down to the bottom where there is a pond and a meadow. It is obvious from the planting schemes that she has a keen eye for colour, and for interesting plants. Much of her inspiration comes from her friend Beth Chatto's garden in East Anglia. The more mature trees and borders are at the top of the slope, from where a brilliant orange-and-red bed catches the eye. Lower down the slope are species roses, unusual shrubs, and hollies. Rambling roses climb through apple trees, and saplings are planted to celebrate new grandchildren and family anniversaries. In front of the house, which has clematis trained up its walls, the terrace has clumps of wind-blown grasses, and the old limestone wall in front is home to small native ferns and lichens.

There is an air of permanence about this garden, of belonging, and it can only get better with time. But there are still new areas to be developed, the most recent being the exciting idea of channelling water down a narrow rill backed by a border of purples and yellows, opposite one of blues and silvers. Opening to the public is a recent venture, but it will not be long before this garden is much better known.

79 High Barn

open	Under NGS, one Sun, Jul, pm, and by appt
directions	SX78 71, A383 Ashburton–Newton Abbot; R to Gale & Burne – to Farlacombe, 2ml top of hill lane on R
owner	Revd I. Graham-Orlebar
address	Hole Farm, nr Bickington, Newton Abbot TQ12 6PE
enquiries	T: 01626 821298 www.holefarm.co.uk

SOUTH

SX78 71

size	1.2h/3a
soil	Light loam
altitude	120m/400ft
aspect	SW
rainfall	89–102cm/35–40in
temperature	Zone C

All the ingredients that go to make a perfect English garden are to be found here in a secluded part of south Devon. The garden surrounds a beautiful farmhouse, parts of which date from the 16th century, and extends down both sides of a sheltered valley. The house was extended a century later, when the outbuildings and barns were constructed. The garden has been in the making since 1992, and its air of great charm is the result of much hard work and knowledgeable planting on the part of the owner. The borders are full of delphiniums, day lilies, hollyhocks, lavender and roses. A weeping willow bends low over the stream, and there is a lily pond, an elderly summerhouse – perfect for tea on warm afternoons – old stone walls, covered with roses, honeysuckle, and clematis, and immaculately kept lawns. On the far side of the valley, paths traverse a natural woodland, above which is a recently planted arboretum, largely of native hardwood species. An old orchard contains some lovely mature trees, which still produce plenty of fruit.

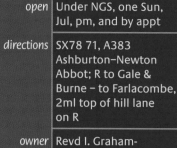

80 Hole Farm

open	Under NGS, one Sun each May, Jun, pm, and by appt
directions	SX54 48, follow Parsonage Road to The Green X, then R into Court Road
owners	Mr & Mrs V. Stevenson
address	Inglewood, 81 Court Road, Newton Ferrers PL8 1BZ
enquiries	T: 01752 872747

SOUTH

SX54 48

size	0.2h/0.75a
soil	Shillet
altitude	60m/18ft
aspect	S, AONB
rainfall	89–102cm/35–40in
temperature	Zone E
	Plant sales

Few sites present such a challenge as this one, overlooking the Yealm Estuary. The roof of the three-storey house is just about level with the top of the garden. Long, steep flights of steps run down alongside the huge retaining wall, constructed in 1902 when the hillside was dug away to accommodate the imposing Edwardian villa. At that time the garden was much larger, but half of it was sold off many years before the Stevensons came here in 1984. Their first move was to create some level areas, connected by narrow paths and steps. Wind can damage plants at the top of the site, but the climate is generally mild and all kinds of exotics flourish, including palms, yuccas, acacias, cordylines, and many unusual shrubs. Patsy Stevenson, a discerning plantswoman, is fond of succulents and grows them both in pots and in the garden. Grass does not feature on such a steep site – there is only one small lawn – but camomile and moss are used to good effect. A splendid *Hydrangea petiolaris* clothes the retaining wall by the house, and there are roses, phlox, jasmine, and magnolia growing among rarer specimens listed on an informative leaflet. The area below the house is less intensively cultivated, being mainly devoted to tall trees, which help to form a windbreak.

81 Inglewood

open	Under NGS, and by appt
directions	SX79 65, from Staverton, due N from Sea Trout Inn, follow signs
owners	Mr & Mrs R. Corfield
address	Kingston House, Staverton, Totnes TQ9 6AP
enquiries	T: 01803 762235 E: info@kingston-estate.demon.co.uk www.kingston-estate.co.uk
EH	House: II*

SOUTH

SX79 65

size	5.2h/13a
soil	Neutral
altitude	50m/175ft
aspect	Level
rainfall	102–114cm/40–45in
temperature	Zone E

Kingston House is a grand mansion dating from 1743, improbably sited amid remote farmland. Three storeys high, square, and somewhat austere in design, it is nonetheless a very elegant building, beautifully finished inside. No expense was spared in its construction – which may be why the owner, John Rowe, went bankrupt. It had a chequered history, ending up as a farmhouse surrounded by agricultural buildings, and a vast expanse of concrete yard. The Corfields bought the property in 1985, and it took several years of hard work to renovate the house to its present state, providing high-class accommodation, cottages, and a popular venue for gatherings. Then it was time to create a garden worthy of, and in keeping with, the house. In came the diggers, and out went the concrete buildings. A garden in the baroque style is planned here, designed to link up with the lime avenue that forms an axis to the house. To the rear of the house are a series of walled gardens, one of which, when cleared of 18in (45cm) of soil, revealed outlines of an original garden. The walls are covered with climbers, and there are formal, box-edged rose-beds. Beyond is a kitchen garden, laid out in patterns both attractive and productive, and an orchard. While the walled entrance courtyard has deliberately been left plain and unplanted, as it should be, the courtyard on the north side is now a charming parterre, with plants producing flowers of soft blues and mauves grouped with silvery-leafed santolinas, and box topiary.

open	Daily, except Wed, am, pm
directions	SX62 51, off A379 Plymouth–Kingsbridge road
owners	Mair & Thompson
address	Mair & Thompson at Flete Walled Gardens, Flete, Ermington, Ivybridge PL21 9NX
enquiries	T: 01752 830100 E: martin@mairand thompson.freeserve. co.uk www. mairandthompson. com

SOUTH

SX62 51

size	2h/5a
soil	Good loam
altitude	61m/200ft
aspect	E, AONB
rainfall	102–114cm/40–45in
temperature	Zone E
	Nursery

In common with other houses of comparable size, the Flete estate aimed to be self-sufficient in fruit and vegetables, and to this end a huge series of glasshouses was constructed behind the house within the shelter of the walled kitchen garden. Unlike most estates, however, Flete still has its glasshouses, although when Glen Mair and Martin Thompson took over in 2000, they were not quite sure what was hidden underneath many years of unchecked growth, left over from the garden's time as a Christmas-tree nursery. Old sale particulars gave details of what had once been there, and it may be that the neglect had a benign effect because, one by one, all the glasshouses, unused and therefore unaltered, have been uncovered. They are exceptional by any standards, and include ranges for peaches, orchids, vines, camellias, and a double-span greenhouse complete with its stove-house and the original pipework.

The largest of the glasshouses is 27m long, and there are three of 18m: each one had to be dug out of the undergrowth, and largely reglazed. They are now used in connection with the nursery business, which specializes in native Chinese species, particularly magnolias, rhododendrons, and peonies.

The next project is the kitchen garden itself. Now cleared of tree roots, it is to be laid out as a physic garden – following the pattern of the original Chelsea Physic Garden – with advice from experts at Chelsea and Kew. The owners consider this to be more interesting than simply recreating a Victorian kitchen garden.

83 Mair & Thompson
at Flete Walled Gardens

open	Under NGS, Mar–Jul, some Sun, pm, and by appt. Please phone
directions	SX60 47, from A379 between Yealmpton and Modbury S to Holbeton, continue 2ml to Mothecombe
owners	Mr & Mrs A. Mildmay-White
address	Mothecombe House, Holbeton PL8 1LA
enquiries	T: 01752 830444
EH	House: I

SOUTH

SX60 47

size	6h/15a
soil	Acid loam, some clay
altitude	60m/200ft
aspect	S, AONB
rainfall	89–102cm/35–40in
temperature	Zone D
	Plant sales

A small peninsula of land bordered by the Erme Estuary and the sea, Mothecombe, with its village of thatched cottages, its own beach and small slipway, and lovely Queen Anne house, has been owned by the same family for four generations. Built of soft grey local stone, with shuttered windows, and a gravel carriage circle surrounded by white railings to the front, the house is almost too good to be true. To one side is the original cross-passage farmhouse, overlooking a walled garden that has been in continuous cultivation for about 300 years. It was here that Anne Mildmay-White started gardening when she moved in as a young bride over 20 years ago. Beyond the walls, the valley drops to the sea. Previous generations planted camellias and rhododendrons here, which are now mature specimens. Many more have been added recently, and new paths – including an avenue of white cherries underplanted with daffodils – and woodland areas developed. The small stream has been dammed to form a pond, and a bog area full of hostas, huge arum lilies, ferns, flag irises, skunk-cabbage, and drifts of primulas. Willows and alders provide a shelterbelt, and higher up, many new trees have been planted, some to re-place those lost in the gales of 1990. Since the woodland has been allowed to grow up, an in-crease in the number of peregrine falcons, buzzards, hawks, and owls has been noticed. At the top of the garden, a new venture has been the planting of over 600 trees, mainly native species, in a wide semi-circle, and from here a path has been cut to the high-est point, providing a wonderful view over the gar-den and the estate. (See also **83 Mothecombe**, 124).

84 Mothecombe House

open	Daily, am, pm
directions	SX72 37, 1.5ml SW of Salcombe follow NT signs
owner	NT
address	Overbecks, Sharpitor, Salcombe, TQ8 8LW
enquiries	T: 01548 842893 E: overbecks@ nationaltrust.org.uk www.nationaltrust. org.uk

SOUTH

SX72 37

EH	Gardens: II
size	2.4h/6a
soil	Slightly alkaline
altitude	30m/100ft
aspect	NE, AONB
rainfall	102–114cm/40–45in
temperature	Zone D
	Plant sales

The large Edwardian house, now a youth hostel and museum, was given to the National Trust in 1937 by Otto Overbeck. When he purchased the property in 1928, the terracing and some of the trees were already there, and he spent the rest of his life enhancing the garden with exotic plants.

The climate of south Devon is so mild that all kinds of tender plants not only survive, but flourish, their lush growth encouraged by the unique microclimate of this steep valley site. Palms and tree ferns, eucalyptus, and the largest camphor tree in the country, olives and mimosa, tall spires of salvias and healthy clumps of agapanthus look very much at home here. Paths winding up and down the site give visitors a chance to see these wonderful specimens from all angles, and to appreciate the size reached by more familiar plants such as fuchsia, hydrangea, grevillea, and cornus. There are glimpses of the sea through the mature trees that provide shelter from the westerly winds. A fine specimen of *Magnolia campbellii*, planted in 1901, is a treat in early March, when it is covered in thousands of deep pink, chalice-shaped flowers. Higher up the site is the Statue Garden, a formal herbaceous area, and the Rock Dell, leading to a lawn with magnificent views.

85 Overbecks

open	1 Apr–mid Oct, daily, am, pm
directions	SX88 69, A380 Exeter–Newton Abbot, follow tourist signs from Penn Inn roundabout
owner	Mr R. Brown
address	Plant World, St Marychurch Road, Newton Abbot TQ12 4SE
enquiries	T: 01803 872939

SOUTH

SX88 69

size	1.7h/4a
soil	Red loam
altitude	90m/300ft
aspect	N, AGLV
rainfall	102–114cm/40–45in
temperature	Zone D
NC	Cortusoides primulas
	Nursery

On a steep, north-facing slope, a remarkable series of gardens has been planned and planted by Ray Brown, representing each of the five continents. The idea took root in 1985 and, as he says, pre-dates Cornwall's Eden Project by some years. A breathtaking display of plants, including many tender and rare species, crowds the hillside. Many of the plants are raised from seed, and at the very bottom of the slope is the trial ground, ablaze with colour and jam-packed with all sorts of interesting new varieties. Many of these find their way into the catalogues of national seed merchants, but Ray Brown also has his own seed catalogue, which lists a huge range and is in great demand. Seven full-time gardeners are kept busy running the nursery, the seed business, and the gardens, all of which are interrelated and mutually supporting. Not surprisingly, Plant World has been featured many times on television and in magazines. A wide range of plants and seeds from around the world is on sale.

Negotiating the network of paths that links the gardens is like finding your way around a maze, and is definitely not for the infirm.

open	Under NGS, twice in Jun
directions	SX65 46 From A379 Plymouth–Kingsbridge, S at Harraton X B3392, R at Pickwick Inn, park Journey's End car-park opposite church
owners	Mr & Mrs J. Bracey
address	Scypen, Ringmore, Kingsbridge TQ7 4HJ
enquiries	T: 01548 810646

SOUTH

SX65 46

size	0.2ha/0.5a
soil	Shallow, pH6–6.5
altitude	90m/300ft
aspect	SW, AONB
rainfall	89–102cm/35–40in
temperature	Zone E

Scypen takes its name from the old cow-shed that the Braceys converted to their home in 1980. The garden is a success-ful combination of hard landscaping and clever planting schemes. The former is the work of John Bracey, a retired archi-tect, who planned the curving walks and beds, the slate-capped walls and con-temporary features of this windswept plateau, all of which were designed to make the most of the views to the coast. The whole garden was planned to be labour-saving, and not something that would demand all of the owners' spare time. Much of the planting is low, to withstand the winds, and very com-pact, offering protection to neighbour-ing plants, and giving weeds little or no chance. The beautiful white cherry 'Mount Fuji' is tolerant of sea winds, and is underplanted with phormiums, sages and silver-foliage plants. This theme is repeated elsewhere in the garden, with many white-flowered shrubs and perennials. Surrounded by thymes and set in a circular bed of pebbles is a modern sun-dial set to local time. Beyond is the garden's most important feature: the Fountain of Life, where a curved wall leads to a series of ponds, the upper one with a fountain based on the double helix. Mathematical ra-

tios have been used in much of the design, including the Millennium wall, which is question-mark-shaped, ending in a world globe. Tender shrubs grow in small, enclosed areas; there is a bronze garden and a cro-quet lawn, beneath which are water storage tanks in readiness for any dramatic climate change.

The great bulk of Dartmoor divides north from south, and east from west Devon. The huge granite mass, formed some 280 million years ago, rises to 610m (2,000ft) in the north. Few roads cross the moor, and habitations are clustered together in the valleys. In winter it can seem forbidding and threatening; in summer it draws thousands of visitors to climb the tors or splash in the streams.

There has been human habitation here since the Stone Age – indeed, Dartmoor has the greatest density of prehistoric remains in north-western Europe – but living has always been hard on the moor. Sheep and ponies survive, but little else. In the Middle Ages pack-horses carried wool between the abbeys at Buckfast and Tavistock, and the granite clapper bridges – of which there is a good example at Postbridge – are part of these routes.

Buckfastleigh was once Devon's most important wool-manufacturing town. The abbey was founded in the 11th century, and abandoned at the dissolution of the monasteries. The present abbey was completed by Benedictine monks in 1937, and stands on the foundations of the original Cistercian building. The peaceful **Abbey Gardens** contain the National Collection of lavenders, a Physic and a Sensory garden.

For a time, precarious and hard-won wealth came from tin found in the streams in sufficient quantities for Dartmoor to merit five stannary towns, where the metal was assayed and traded. Copper deposits were found near Tavistock, and the profits from this trade greatly increased the wealth of the Russell family who owned much of the town and were largely responsible for its development. The public gardens alongside the river are pleasant; also worth a visit is the old burial ground bordering the back road to the north, with some fine trees and a carpet of bulbs in the spring.

In the southern part of Dartmoor, the landscape is less severe, and the climate milder. The valleys are longer and deeper, with greater tree cover and woodlands.

6 DARTMOOR

The moist air and shelter afforded by the valleys encourages lush growth, and here some fine gardens have flourished – **Heathercombe** (95), **Endsleigh** (4), and **The Garden House** (5), for example – in conditions that are ideal for rhododendrons.

Dartmoor has been a National Park since 1951, and within its confines are some strange bedfellows. The Park and the National Trust each own some 3,500 acres (1,418ha), and the Nature Conservancy Council over 17,000 acres (6,885ha). All these have a common aim, and are often at odds with the Ministry of Defence

(over 13,000 acres/5,265ha), the Forestry Commission (some 1,750 acres/710ha), and the Water Authority (3,600 acres/ 1,458ha). Development of any kind – reservoirs, roads, telecommunication masts – is greeted with massive opposition. The presence of the military is contentious, as is the vast workings of china clay on the southern edges of the moor. Most of the summer visitors to Dartmoor are completely unaware of such issues, and come only to enjoy the beauty of the scenery. They bring much needed income, and Dartmoor would be impoverished without this annual influx.

open	Under NGS, some Sat, May, Jun, pm; Jul, some evenings, and by appt
directions	SX62 93, turn L in village by common
owners	Mr & Mrs R.J. Hill
address	Andrew's Corner, Belstone EX20 1RD
enquiries	T: 01837 840332 E: edwina-robin. hill@virgin.net

DARTMOOR

SX62 93

size	0.6ha/1.5a
soil	Acid, thin
altitude	300m/1,000ft
aspect	N, Dartmoor Nat Park
rainfall	140–153cm/50–60in
temperature	Zone G
	Plant sales

Mr and Mrs Hill senior retired to Belstone in 1967, coming to a house with little garden, but superb views over the valley of the River Taw, known here as Skaigh Warren, across to the great height of Cawsand Beacon. Much as they would have liked to keep the view, shelter from cruel winds was essential if anything was to grow here, more than 300m up on Dartmoor. Careful siting and choice of trees allow glimpses of Dartmoor, so that the garden is not entirely shut away. The early garden consisted of conifers and beds of heathers, which were fashionable at that time, along with a good selection of *Acer* and birch.

By the time Robin Hill, with his family, joined his father here in 1979, much of this early planting had either outgrown its space or was past its best, so some clearing was necessary. Very few conifers remain, and no heathers: in their place are magnolias, specimen trees such as the tulip tree, and more silver birch and *Acer*, which do very well here. Spring is a particularly beautiful season in this garden, as everything is underplanted with bulbs and low-growing perennials. There are beds of rhododendrons, and two ponds to attract wildlife, with which the garden abounds. The colourful herbaceous borders are relatively new, and include agapanthus intermixed with grasses. A new area is devoted to alpines and autumn-flowering gentians.

The garden first opened to the public in 1972, and has been open regularly since then. In 2003 it was one of the first to try evening openings, with over 130 candles in lamps throughout the garden, in the trees and flowerbeds, adding an air of enchantment.

88 Andrew's Corner

open	Early Jul, 1 Sat, Sun, pm, all year by appt
directions	SX65 94, walk through churchyard
owners	Mr & Mrs R. Yeates
address	Blackhall Manor South Tawton EX20 2LP
enquiries	T: 01837 840171
EH	House: II

DARTMOOR

SX65 94

P.

size	Small
soil	Neutral
altitude	190m/666ft
aspect	NE, Dartmoor Nat Park
rainfall	114–127cm/50–55in
temperature	Zone F
	Plant sales

A walk across the churchyard takes visitors to the 16th-century thatched Devon longhouse. Little of **Blackhall Manor**'s original garden, never very grand, survives: the Yeates, who have been here since 1987, have created the present garden (right). Don't be fooled into thinking that the cobbled paths and courtyard are original – all were laid by Roger Yeates. It is his wife who has the eye for colour that is so evident throughout. Everywhere are lovely combinations: the whole garden is bursting with good ideas and inspiration for visitors. Many of the plants are raised in the greenhouse, and every year a few subtle changes are made in the garden as plants outgrow their allotted spaces, or Jacqueline Yeates has fresh ideas. There is a wide variety of planting in the different areas of the garden: particularly effective use is made of climbers on trellises and arches, and of groups of plants in pots.

Also open with Blackhall Manor are two gardens at Sticklepath, backing on to the River Taw as it rushes off Dartmoor. **Taw Bank** has interesting herbaceous borders and a viewing platform looking over the river, the banks of which have been terraced to grow vegetables and soft fruit. Its neighbour, **Taw Meadow**, is larger – 0.66 acres (0.27ha) – with a shady area by the river, and a silver birch glade. There are dry areas on the slope, which is planted with numerous varieties of ornamental grasses, and many clematis throughout.

89 Blackhall Manor, Taw Bank & Taw Meadow

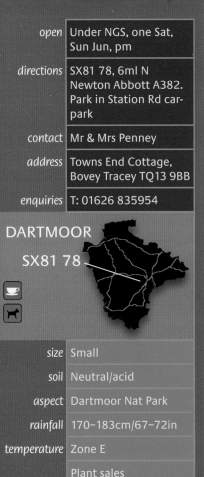

DARTMOOR

SX81 78

size	Small
soil	Neutral/acid
aspect	Dartmoor Nat Park
rainfall	170–183cm/67–72in
temperature	Zone E
	Plant sales

Since at least the 1970s, some half dozen gardens in the Dartmoor town of Bovey Tracey have opened to the public for one weekend in June. Between them they raise over £2,000 for charity, from entrance money, plant sales, and teas. Mostly small in size, the gardens offer a tremendous variety, and good lessons in making the most of a limited area.

At **Brook Lodge** (below right) an explosion of red and pink climbing roses screens the garden from the road, and forms a backdrop to the stream, the margins of which are densely planted. Bedding plants are the thing here, and every inch of this very small garden is utilized. Next door, at **Towns End Cottage**, the owners have completely renovated a derelict house and garden, creating a peaceful, well-designed oasis, complete with pond and several sitting areas. Nearby is **Hillrise** (below), where the owners have gardened since the early 1990s, making the most of the damp, level site with arches and arbours, long borders, and many roses.

At the top of the town, with views out over Dartmoor, the owner of **Hillview** (top left) describes his steep garden as 'a mix of cultivated chaos', with a pond, an orchard, and some woodland. At **2 Devon House Drive** (top right), an intriguing garden has been created by two artistic owners since 1995. It is full of good colour combinations and all sorts of ideas that make it seem a lot larger than it is. A very productive soft fruit and vegetable area produces enough for the family – and the birds. Edges to the beds are made from interwoven apple prunings, keeping the mulching in place, and saving the need to trim the edges of the lawn.

90 Bovey Tracey Gardens

Daily, am, pm

SX72 90, 5ml S of A30, 12ml W of Exeter

NT

Castle Drogo, Drewsteignton EX6 6PB

T: 01647 433306
E: castledrogo@nationaltrust.org.uk
www.nationaltrust.org.uk

House: I

Gardens: II

5ha/12a

Acid shale, stone, over rock

263m/883ft

N, Dartmoor Nat Park

114cm/45in

Zone E

Plant centre

The usual reason for visiting this spectacular National Trust property is to marvel at the granite castle designed by Sir Edwin Lutyens, perched on an outcrop high up the valley of the River Teign.

A long drive approaches the castle, bordered by wide grass verges and holm oaks – *Quercus ilex* – and ending in a gravel forecourt surrounded by clipped yew hedges. Planted on the steep slopes beyond is the spring garden: colourful in season, with massed rhododendrons and flowering trees, it is a garden in the woodland style. This is in direct contrast to the area laid out in about 1927, when the castle was nearing completion. The planting schemes were the work of George Dillestone, but the layout is in the Lutyens tradition, with eastern overtones in the corner pavilions where *Parrotia persica* is trained to form arching canopies. The gardens are unified with yew hedges, and contain formal beds and a sunken rose garden. Terraces climb the hillside, connected with flights of granite steps leading to the Fragrant Garden, where the axial view shows off Haytor and Easden Tor. From the Fragrant Garden, a path between borders of azaleas, magnolias, and cherries leads to a pair of conifers standing sentinel at the top. Looking back the garden is not visible, and the path appears to drop straight down to the gate in the bottom yew hedge. It is a masterly stroke, and would indicate that Lutyens intended visitors to approach from the top. The grass circle at the highest point, again enclosed by yew, is used for croquet.

91 Castle Drogo

open	Under NGS, one Sat, Sun, Sep, pm, and by appt
directions	SX67 88, from A30 take A382 Moretonhampstead via Whiddon Down; R to Gidleigh, adjacent church
owners	Mr & Mrs M. Bell
address	Castle Farm, Gidleigh, Chagford TQ13 8HR
enquiries	T: 01647 433470

DARTMOOR

SX67 88

size	2.8ha/7a
soil	Acid
altitude	300m/900ft
aspect	S
rainfall	140–153cm/55–60in
temperature	Zone D

On the edge of Dartmoor is a tiny hamlet of a few cottages, a small church, and the ruined castle that has given its name to this property. Castle Farm lies in the shadow of the granite church. Developed from a muddy field since 1992, this is a cottage garden that blends in well with the countryside: foxgloves and other wild flowers are allowed to seed themselves freely. Around the house are well-chosen plants that will withstand the damp and cold of a Dartmoor garden. Water forms an important feature in the garden: along the stream that borders it are many moisture-loving plants. On the far side is an arboretum that covers the hillside and contains a collection of *Acer*, various dogwoods, and the rare and beautiful *Quercus robur* 'Raba'.

A stepped, woodland path, planted with ferns and other shade-lovers, leads down to the dark and ivy-hung water. Follow the water upstream to a six-acre (2.4ha) secret valley, where badger, deer, snipe, and the occasional kingfisher can be seen.

92 Castle Farm

open	Under NGS, some days Mar, Jun
directions	SX54 63, park in village, 100yd down lane, opposite church
owners	R.J. Hubble & S.M. Tracey
address	Dippers, Shaugh Prior PL7 5HA
enquiries	T: 01752 839407

DARTMOOR

SX54 63

size	0.3ha/0.75a
soil	Loam pH6
altitude	180m/600ft
aspect	S, Dartmoor Nat Park
rainfall	140–153cm/55–60in
temperature	Zone E
NC	*Dianthus* – dwarf species
	Plant sales

For those who love hellebores, a visit to Dippers is a must in March. Stella Tracey has become something of an expert in this genus, raising large numbers of hellebores each year, which she sells in aid of charity. In a shady area of her garden, several large beds are devoted to innumerable varieties of hellebores in a surprisingly wide variety of colours, all flowering abundantly from January to April. Stella Tracey began with a collection of seed from Will McLewin. Every spring she collects selected seed in little muslin bags made by her mother: in the first year she ended up with 500 seedlings. These are then grown on until they fill a three-litre pot, when they are sold. There is a waiting list for some of the rare varieties that produce very dark flowers. Throughout the garden there are drifts of spring-flowering bulbs, with many different varieties of snowdrop. The garden also has interesting collections of dwarf rhododendrons and conifers.

Stella Tracey's second passion is for *Dianthus*, of which she has about 500 different varieties. These form a National Collection, and she is currently trying to categorize the plants correctly. Many of them are grown on the sunny bank to the rear of her house, a lovely sight when they are all in flower. This area is also where she grows a large number of alpine plants in raised beds and troughs, with the more tender treasures in a glasshouse.

93 Dippers

open	Under NGS, some Sun Jun, pm
directions	SX65 79, B3212 Postbridge, next to church. Park at village hall
owners	Mr & Mrs K. Doyle
address	Drury Head Cottage, Postbridge PL20 6SY
enquiries	T: 01822 880237

DARTMOOR

SX65 79

size	0.4ha/1a
soil	Acid; well-drained peat
altitude	300m/1,000ft
aspect	NW slope, Dartmoor Nat Park
rainfall	183–196cm/70–80in
temperature	Zone G
	Plant sales

This must be one of the last cottages to be 'raised in a day', if the story told to the present owners is to be believed: in 1870 the chimney of Drury Head Cottage was built from hearth to pot in a single day to establish ownership of the land. The cottage is adjacent to the church, and to one side is a narrow lane leading up on to Dartmoor. The climate is milder than might be expected of such a situation. Jenny Doyle came from Essex, so found gardening on Dartmoor a new challenge: the rate of growth, once plants are established, still surprises her. With great enthusiasm, the Doyles began their garden in 1994, and already it has an established air.

The garden is long and narrow, surrounded by trees that provide shelter. This area was broken up with beds planted to provide year-round interest. The front garden is more formal, and the raised beds of gritty soil for growing alpines are a new venture. Jenny Doyle favours little plants, and has a particular fondness for alpines. Another scree bed behind the house is covered with violets, and is full of spring bulbs, anemones and cyclamen. Jenny Doyle is one of the growing number of organic gardeners, and her vegetable and fruit areas flourish to the extent of leaving her with surplus produce to sell locally. She has also begun propagating her plants for sale. In the wild-flower meadow at the top, where butterfly orchids thrive, are her pet geese and donkeys – and Izzie, the pot-belly pig, who attracts a great deal of attention on open days.

94 Drury Head Cottage

open	Under NGS, last Sun Mar, two Sun May, one Sun Jun, Oct, pm
directions	SX71 81, at Heatree X on B3344 take lane towards Natsworthy through stone pillars
owner	Claude & Margaret Pike Woodlands Trust
address	Heathercombe Woodland Garden, Manaton TQ13 9XE
enquiries	T: 01647 221222

DARTMOOR

SX71 81

size	8ha/20a in larger woodland
soil	Lime-free
altitude	320m/1,050ft
aspect	Open, Dartmoor Nat Park
rainfall	180cm/71in
temperature	Zone G

Heathercombe Woodland Garden is an extensive estate developed since 1966 by the late Claude Pike as a haven for wildlife. The valley is full of history, and includes a Devon long-house and bronze age hut circles. Woodland walks have been created beside the many streams and ponds, and an arboretum of native and exotic species, many of which give fine autumn colour. There are over 500 labelled species of trees and shrubs throughout the valley and woodland gardens. An orchard of Devon varieties has been planted, and a wildflower meadow is becoming established. In spring many areas are covered with flowering bulbs, including bluebells, with many rhododendrons and azaleas.

95 Heathercombe Woodland Garden

open	Under NGS, end Mar–end May, Sun, Bank Holiday Mon, pm, and by appt
directions	SX79 80, A382 Bovey Tracey–Moretonhampstead, L to Lustleigh, 0.25ml L R, 0.25ml up steep drive
owners	Rosemary & David Quicke
address	Higher Knowle, Lustleigh, Newton Abbott TQ13 9SP
enquiries	T: 01647 277275 E: d.quicke@ connectfree.co.uk

DARTMOOR

SX79 80

size	1.2ha/3a
soil	Poor, thin, pH 5.5
altitude	137m/450ft
aspect	SW slope
rainfall	114–127cm/45–50in
temperature	Zone F
	Plant sales

From early March to mid-June the slopes of this three-acre (1.2 ha), granite-strewn garden are a delight to all lovers of rhododendrons and magnolias. Even earlier, when spared by frost, are the fluttering pink and white blossoms of *Magnolia sprengeri* and *M. denudata*, planted long ago. Large numbers of camellias flower around the house, which merges perfectly with the hillside behind, being built of granite, with a low curving roof-line – it was originally thatched.

Since 1955, Higher Knowle been owned successively by two keen gardeners. The first, Miss Goater, planted many of the magnolias and most of the woodland, and would only sell to the Quickes after they had convinced her of their gardening knowledge and skills. They took over in 1965, and Miss Goater moved across the road.

The trees create the ideal setting for the woodland garden of rhododendrons, and for the bluebells and primroses that carpet the ground. Each new addition is carefully noted, with date and place of purchase: the list includes over 50 magnolias, 17 acers, and hundreds of rhododendrons. Closer to the house, where mature beech hedges create windbreaks, are flowering cherries, a mimosa hedge, and a rockery bed. Lustleigh Vale is normally blessed with a mild climate, but occasionally hard frosts do great damage, and lately strong winds and heavy rainfall have caused mature trees to come crashing down. Being a true gardener, David Quicke sees this as an opportunity either to let in more light, or to plant new species in the space created.

96 Higher Knowle

open	End Mar, early Apr, Sun, pm; mid-Apr–mid-Jun, Sun, Wed, Bank Holiday Mon, pm, and by appt
directions	SX64 58, off A38 at Ivybridge, N to Harford
owner	Mrs R. Howell
address	Lukesland, Ivybridge PL21 0JF
enquiries	T: 01752 893390
EH	House: II

DARTMOOR

SX64 58

size	6ha/15a
soil	Acid
altitude	200m/800ft
aspect	SW slope, Dartmoor Nat Park
rainfall	153–170cm/60–65in
temperature	Zone F

Situated on the southern edge of Dartmoor, the gardens at Lukesland are surprisingly lush: tall palm trees bend in the wind, and rare conifers have grown to great heights. Running through the garden, and forming one of its principal features, is a rushing Dartmoor stream. Its margins are planted with primulas and ferns, and it feeds large ponds before cascading down between steep rocky banks.

The imposing Victorian house, built in 1862, has been owned by the Howell family since the 1930s. Brian Howell, who died in 2003, was a forester: one of his first projects on inheriting Lukesland was a pinetum, which added yet more interesting species to the garden. The original Victorian layout of paths, stone steps, and bridges remains largely unchanged. This is primarily a spring garden, with banks of Exbury hybrid azaleas, and rhododendrons creating a stunning display from mid-April to mid-June. Camellias have been planted on the wooded banks, and wild flowers are allowed to run riot: wood anemones, bluebells, drifts of red campion and herb robert, and cheerful yellow Welsh poppies are all regarded as friends of the garden.

Two prized specimen trees are a 17m *Davidia involucrata* planted in 1936, which never fails to produce thousands of fluttering white bracts in late May, and a *Magnolia campbellii*, one of the largest specimens in the country, which is an unforgettable sight in March when its bare branches are covered with pink flowers. Nearby is the white-flowered variety; both were planted in 1936.

open	Mid-May–end Sep, daily, pm
directions	SX70 90, from A382 Whiddon Down–Moretonhampstead, L to Drewsteignton, 2nd R
owners	Mr & Mrs K. Ashburner
address	Stone Farm, Stone Lane, Chagford TQ13 8JU
enquiries	T: 01647 231311 E: mythicgarden@talk21.com www.mythicgarden.com
EH	House: II

DARTMOOR

SX70 90

P P₊ ♿
👥 📖 🐕 ⛩

size	2ha/5a
soil	Acid, heavy
altitude	250m/800ft
aspect	S, Dartmoor Nat Park
rainfall	127–140cm/50–55in
temperature	Zone F
NC	Birch, Alder
	Nursery

Tree trunks, water, rustling leaves, and a patchwork of greens act as the setting for a changing exhibition of sculpture. There are surprises round every corner for visitors walking through this garden-gallery. Each year in the spring about 100 pieces of sculpture, ranging from large groups of figures, to small pieces perched in and around the ponds and stream, are displayed at Stone Farm. This is the 'mythic' element of the garden: the arboretum was originally conceived and planted in 1971, as a scientific test area. Kenneth Ashburner turned a field of stodgy soil into a trial ground for different varieties of birch and alder – species in which he is now an acknowledged expert. He has always been involved in horticulture, and has travelled widely, collecting seed from all over the world, which was then raised at Stone Farm. Initially, the trees were planted out in blocks for purposes of comparison. The underplanting, among which a specially developed rubus – *Rubus* 'Kenneth Ashburner' – is used to good effect, was kept deliberately simple. As the trees matured, the Ashburners realized that their trial ground was special: Kenneth Ashburner has described it as 'an art form – there is movement, swaying of foliage, sound from leaves, aroma from buds and flowers, and ever changing perspective.' It was at this stage that the idea of an outdoor sculpture exhibition began to take shape. June Ashburner had previously run an art gallery in Chagford, so it seemed an obvious step to combine gardening and art. It is a combination that has proved highly popular.

98 Mythic Garden

open	Under NGS, and by appt – gardens and nursery
directions	SX47 81, Lydford–Tavistock road (NOT A386), take Liddaton road, Lydford side of Brentor Inn. 300yd on R
owners	Mr & Mrs J. Carter
address	Rowden Gardens, Brentor, Tavistock PL19 0NG
enquiries	T: 01822 810275

DARTMOOR

SX47 81

size	0.4h/1a
soil	Neutral–acid
altitude	200m/800ft
aspect	Level, N/S, Dartmoor Nat Park
rainfall	127–140cm/50–55in
temperature	Zone F
NC	*Polygonum*; Water Iris; *Ranunculus ficaria*; *Caltha*
	Nursery

Rowden Gardens is the place to visit if you want to learn about water gardening and plants that love damp soil. Do not go if you are in a hurry, for here you should walk slowly, and look, listen, and learn. Ten parallel canals, divided by grass paths and borders of unusual trees and shrubs, are planted with a huge collection of plants, including four different National Collections – of *Caltha*, *Polygonum*, *Ranunculus ficaria*, and, most attractive of them all, Water Iris. John Carter has specialized in aquatic plants since the 1980s, and is an acknowledged expert in the field. The author of countless gardening articles, he has judged for the RHS; has exhibited regularly at the RHS Chelsea Flower Show, and is a veteran of major shows and television programmes.

As well as its National Collections for the NCCPG, the nursery and gardens contain important displays of *Iris ensata*, ferns, *Rodgersia*, *Ligularia*, and water-lilies. A very major contribution to horticulture has been the large number of new hybrids, particularly irises, that have been produced here.

99 Rowden Gardens

open	Under NGS, Sun end May–end Jun, and by appt
directions	SX71 76, SW from village past church, 200 yd R to Southcombe
owners	Dr & Mrs J.R. Seale
address	Southcombe House, Widecombe-in-the-Moor TQ13 7TU
enquiries	T: 01364 621365
EH	House: II

DARTMOOR

SX71 76

size	2ha/5a
soil	Thin, sandy, neutral on granite
altitude	270m/900ft highest point
aspect	SE slope, Dartmoor Nat Park
rainfall	153–170cm/60–65in
temperature	Zone G

Wild-flower gardening has become fashionable in recent years. Here, on a steeply sloping Dartmoor hillside, Dr Seale has been doing it since the early 1990s. He was already retired when he moved to the lovely Devon longhouse, and had few plans for gardening other than the area in front of the house. But when he acquired the four-acre (1.6ha) former meadow, partly planted with trees and shrubs ten years earlier, but then neglected, all that changed. With a 'gleam of inspiration', as he puts it, he cleared a smallish area – bare earth is essential – and scattered over it bales of hay cut from two of the few remaining ancient meadows in Dartmoor National Park that have not been 'agriculturally improved'. Two summers later he was rewarded with a drift of ox-eye daisies, and from this modest beginning he has now converted almost the entire acreage. As the wild flowers become established, new varieties keep appearing, including several orchid species. In a few cases, Dr Seale has helped nature, but by and large all seed came out of the hay bales, followed by self-seeding. It is not surprising that would-be wild-flower gardeners beat a path to his door, and Dr Seale readily gives advice, and in 2002 sold several of his own hay bales to local enthusiasts. It is a very relaxed way of gardening: grass-cutting is left until August, apart from a few grass paths winding through the meadow, and ceases in October; there is no weeding to be done, no edges to trim, and pruning takes place as and when it is required. Meanwhile, there is a wonderful abundance of wildlife to watch. The considerable bonus of this site, 275m above sea level, is the backdrop of mature trees, beyond the open moor and tors.

100 Southcombe House

DARTMOOR

SX83 88

size	2ha/5a
soil	Light shillet
altitude	50–150m/190–500ft
aspect	SSW, AGLV
rainfall	89–102cm/35–40in
temperature	Zone E
	Plant sales

Bordered on one side by the River Teign, and on the other by the old mill leat, the four-acre (1.6ha) gardens of Sowton Mill naturally abound in moisture-loving plants. Here is a large cottage garden crammed with choice plants, including *Acer*, *Buddleja*, *Clematis*, *Cornus*, *Diascia*, *Symphytum*, and *Magnolia*, lovingly tended by two devoted gardeners, one of whom – Sonia Newton – was brought up at Sowton. The earliest plants were brought home from continental holidays by her grandfather, and have flourished in the mild climate; but gardening proper had to wait until the owners retired in the late 1980s. Since then, the garden has developed in a charmingly haphazard way. The paths wind between borders packed with *Dierama*, *Hosta*, *Primula*, *Euphorbia*, and *Vinca* (periwinkle), past an *Exochorda*, and on under the shade of specimen trees – an early planting now reaching a splendid maturity. Further along the leat are spectacular shrub roses, and there is room for the mighty ramblers 'Kiftsgate', 'Rambling Rector', and 'Wedding Day' to reach their full potential. The plants at Sowton are meticulously recorded, and the long list makes impressive reading.

The garden is long and narrow, but an area of woodland above the mill cottages has been taken in, and planted with rhododendrons and woodland shrubs. A steep path through the trees gives views back over the cottages and the Teign valley. Here the bluebells and wild garlic run riot, while in early spring a carpet of crocuses, wild daffodils and wood anemones clothes the river bank: the informal, semi-wild atmosphere is encouraged. The garden seems to be a small, private world, but one to which visitors can return again and again – not least because of the wide range of 'surplus plants' offered for sale.

101 Sowton Mill

open	Under NGS; groups strictly by appt; please ring for details
directions	SX75 86, 0.5ml N of village on A382, R at derestriction sign
owners	Mr & Mrs E. Allhusen
address	Sutton Mead, Moretonhampstead TQ13 8PW
enquiries	T: 01647 440296

DARTMOOR

SX75 86

P

size	1.2ha/3a
soil	pH 5.5
altitude	230m/750ft
aspect	E, Dartmoor Nat Park
rainfall	117cm/46in
temperature	Zone F
	Plant sales

With a busy publishing business, and the NGS, which she helps to organize, it is a wonder that Miranda Allhusen has time to garden at all. The older areas of the garden include banks of rhododendrons and azaleas, and the pond, where a seat is placed to take advantage of the view across fields to Mardon Down. Other areas have been developed as family circumstances have changed: a round pond and rill were constructed in the woodland; a silver wedding anniversary resulted in the planting of a bed of white roses; and what was the donkey field is now a young arboretum. Two rugby-playing sons, and a husband with a passion for building granite walls, have greatly helped. This formidable team was called in when Miranda Allhusen decided to redesign the former kitchen yard to the rear of the house: a new retaining wall with flights of steps, and a water-filled trough, combined with imaginative planting is the happy result. The very top of the garden is a recent acquisition, and is being nurtured as a wild garden – nettles, brambles, and docks are removed to allow campions, cow parsley, foxgloves, and bluebells to flourish. A vegetable plot has been worked into the overall scheme of the garden.

An unusual greenhouse with arched concrete struts had fallen into such a state of disrepair that it was going to be demolished. Happily, Edward Allhusen decided to repair it – a task that involved major rebuilding work. Although the reglazing caused problems, the effort has paid off in the finished result, which is a source of great admiration.

open	Under NGS, some Sun May, Jun, pm
directions	SX61 93, fork L at stocks in village, 300 yd on R
owners	Mr & Mrs R. Bernays
address	Taikoo, Belstone, Okehampton EX20 1QZ
enquiries	T: 01837 840217

DARTMOOR

SX61 93

size	1ha/2.5a
soil	Stoney, acid
altitude	330m/1,100ft
aspect	SSE, Dartmoor Nat Park
rainfall	170–183cm/65–70in
temperature	Zone G

Built in 1924 on a lovely moorland site by the Taipan of Swires, the great Hong Kong trading company, this is one of the most extraordinary houses in Devon. The Taipan and his descendants lived at Taikoo for 70 years, but by the time the Bernays took over the property in 1995, the house needed major refurbishment, and the garden was a neglected wilderness. Both of the Bernays had gardening mothers, and were brought up in an atmosphere of plants and gardening talk. They decided to create a new garden on this wonderful site, with its far-reaching views of Dartmoor and mid-Devon. With help from Pippa Irwin, the rough grass and scrub disappeared, to be replaced by terraces, beds, ponds, steps, shady areas full of hostas, and an enormous number of roses around the house – which Mrs Bernay was told wouldn't grow on Dartmoor. In the spring, 300 dwarf rhododendrons, set off with drifts of bulbs and fritillaries, make a ribbon of colour through the garden. An arboretum has been planted on the hillside, which rises to a summerhouse: this is an ideal spot for taking advantage of the views. Wind damage is a problem that has been solved with shelterbelts of conifers and tall shrubs, and a long, snaking, woven fence.

103 Taikoo

open	Under NGS, one Sun each, May, Sep, pm
directions	SX81 79, from A382 take road signed Hospital, after 0.3ml turn L, private road to Whitstone Vineyard, farm on R
owners	Mr & Mrs A. Bunn
address	Whitstone Farm, Bovey Tracey TQ13 9NA
enquiries	T: ex directory

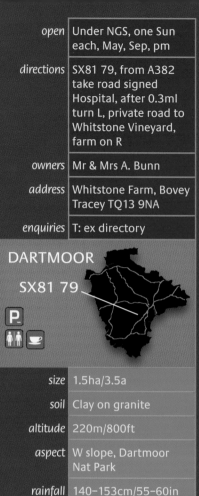

DARTMOOR

SX81 79

size	1.5ha/3.5a
soil	Clay on granite
altitude	220m/800ft
aspect	W slope, Dartmoor Nat Park
rainfall	140–153cm/55–60in
temperature	Zone F

A medieval farm once occupied this three-acre (1.2ha) site, high above Bovey Tracey, with magnificent views to Trendlebere Down and Haytor on the skyline. The original house has long since disappeared, and what the Bunns bought in 1999 was a barn converted in 1900. They had no idea that there had ever been a garden on the steep hillside behind them: not until they began tentatively to clear the bank did they realize that someone had been there before. Terraces and paths emerged, and clearance of the undergrowth revealed mature trees and shrubs, which were certainly not native species. All this had been abandoned by the previous owners, the Cooks, who had grown too old and infirm to cope with the garden that they had laid out in the early 1970s, and planted with 280 specimen trees, including eucalyptus, mimosa, magnolia, and many rare varieties of sorbus, alder, horse-chestnut, and pine – some as yet unidentified.

In just four years, Katie and Alan Bunn revived the garden, with very little outside help. They have planted the area around the house with roses, shrubs and plenty of plants in pots, and have recently added the cascade and pool. Beyond is the original arboretum, to which the Bunns have added some new planting. Very few of the old trees retained their labels, so tree experts are always welcome here.

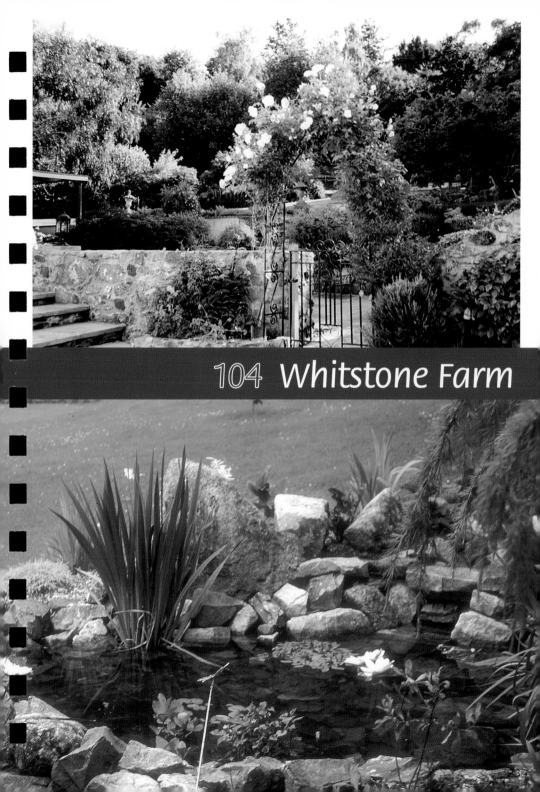

104 Whitstone Farm

open	Under NGS, early May Sun, Bank Holiday Mon, pm
directions	SX67 57, midway between Ivybridge and South Brent on old A 38, N at Blacksmith Lane
owners	Surg. Capt. & Mrs R. Travis
address	Wrangaton House, Wrangaton TQ10 9HH
enquiries	T: 01364 72104
EH	House: II

DARTMOOR

SX67 57

size	2ha/5a
soil	Acid, pH7
altitude	190m/650ft
aspect	SSE, Dartmoor Nat Park
rainfall	152cm/60in
temperature	Zone F
	Plant sales

The southern slopes of Dartmoor form a backdrop to the 18th-century house, built on the site of a medieval manor, the ruined kitchen of which adjoins the house. This is a much-loved family home, and in the garden harmonious borders, rather than specialist plant collections, are favoured, particularly around the large croquet lawn where opera evenings are staged in summer. The pond, which attracts mallards and dragonflies, is fed by a small, leat-like stream, its banks planted with primulas and lilies. Beyond is a ha-ha, with views over the fields across the South Hams to the sea. In spring – Marjorie Travis's favourite season – drifts of white daffodils line the drive under a canopy of white cherry blossom and magnolias. Around the lawn, white camellias echo the planting scheme. Visitors are welcome to walk in the adjoining bluebell woods. Gaily planted pots line the old stone walls of the house and outbuildings, and climbers soften the outlines. A hidden herb garden has been cleverly planted in a small enclosure beside the house. Marjorie Travis also keeps bees, so many of the shrubs have been chosen for their benefit: the clipped cotoneaster around the porch is particularly popular. Many visitors come whenever the garden is open, to enjoy the peaceful surroundings, strolling among trees and shrubs.

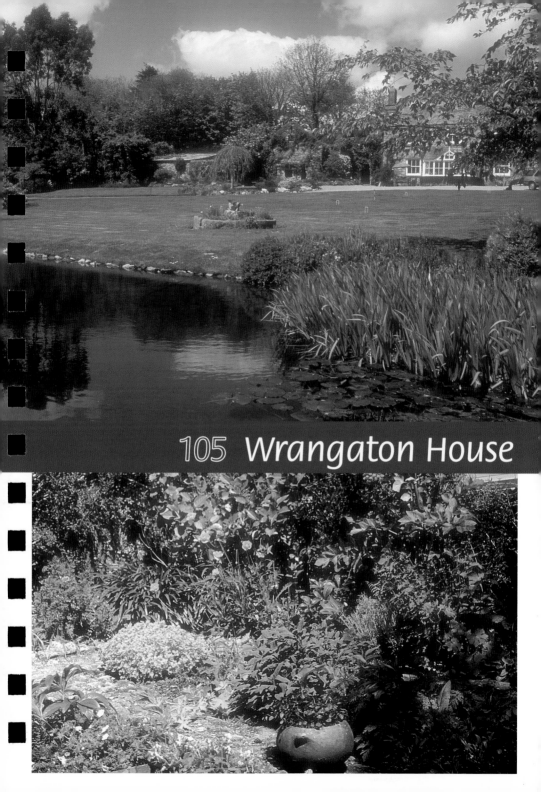

105 Wrangaton House

This book is a guide to gardens that are reliably open to the public. However, a number of gardens in Devon open occasionally, but not on a regular basis. Some are nurseries with gardens, where the main interest is the nursery; others are gardens that open as an adjunct to another business. Still others are gardens that have opened to the public only recently, including a number that are still being reclaimed after years of neglect.

They are mentioned below in order to complete the gazetteer. Opening times are advertised in local papers; on local radio programmes, and by the NGS. The monthly magazine *Inside Devon*, and the two free papers *The Devon Country Gardener* and *The Devon Gardener*, which can be found in nurseries, all contain up-to-date information.

These gardens are numbered in sequence with those in the main gazetteer.

7 *Additional Gardens Open to the Public*

NORTH

106 Broomhill Sculpture Gardens
Muddiford, Barnstaple EX31 4EX
T: 01271 850262; E: Info@broomhillart.co.uk.
Open: May–Oct, Wed–Sun, am, pm; Nov–Apr, Thur–Sun, pm

The sculpture park in the grounds of Broomhill Hotel was begun in 1997, after a massive clearance of overgrown woodland. Throughout the ten acres (4ha) are a wide variety of sculptures, some permanent, but most for sale – the work of over 60 artists.

A huge scarlet stiletto shoe greets the visitor on the terrace overlooking the woodland, and the majority of the works

are contemporary in style. Paths and steps lead through the grounds, which are mostly natural woodland with wild flowers and native trees. The Victorian hotel also houses an art gallery.

107 Chambercombe Manor
Chambercombe Lane, Ilfracombe EX34 9RJ
T: 01271 862624 ; www.chambercombemanor.co.uk
Open Easter–Oct, Mon–Fri, am, pm; Sun, pm

In a secluded, wooded valley is Chambercombe Manor. The manor is recorded in the 'Domesday Book', but the present house dates from the 16th century. Both the house and grounds are said to be haunted. The latter are being reclaimed after a period of neglect. Lawns border the stream that feeds two large ponds – the haunt of ducks and wildfowl. A 'silent pool' is fed by a spring, and is surrounded by mature woodland. Flowering bulbs, camellias, rhododendrons and magnolias are followed by roses, herbaceous borders, and hydrangeas in summer, then by autumn colour.

108 Chapel Farm House
Mr & Mrs R. Hull, Chapel Farm House, Halwill Junction, Beaworthy EX21 5UF
T: 01409 221594
Open: Apr–Sep, some Sun, am, pm

Robin Hull and his Japanese wife Toshie began their nursery at Chapel Farm in 1998. Everything they sell is propagated and raised on the site, and they specialize in herbaceous plants. Their own garden is laid out with broad beds of rhododendrons, azaleas, and heathers, and is structured around plantings of small trees. A new venture is an alpine bed, with the plants in pots so that they can be moved into the greenhouse (right) if necessary. At one end, beneath a eucalyptus planted in 1993, is a pond that dries out in summer, but which still supports much wildlife. The house, which dates from 1641, was an inn before it was shut down in 1892, for 'rowdy behaviour' on the part of the customers. Sheltering behind it is a collection of bonsai, and some unusual, tender pot plants.

109 Clovelly Court Garden

Clovelly Court Garden, Clovelly, nr Bideford EX39 5SZ
T: 01237 431781

Open Apr–Oct

Clovelly Court, the manor house next to the church, presides over the picturesque village. To the south of the house are the extensive kitchen gardens, recently restored and replanted, and now open to the public. Around the walls are espaliered fruit trees, and this area is a productive organic market garden. The long, lean-to greehouse, complete with its original lever mechanism, houses apricots, peaches, vines and figs, as well as more tender species. Two further greenhouses are devoted to tomatoes, and there is an ornamental garden with herbaceous borders and orchard trees. The gardens around the Court are not open.

110 The Gate House

Mr & Mrs D. Booker, The Gate House, Lee, Ilfracombe EX34 8LR
T: 01271 862409; www.leebay.co.uk

Open: Most days, under NGS; essential to phone first

Over two acres (0.8ha) worked organically, only a few minutes' walk from the sea. Peaceful streamside garden with a range of habitats: bog garden; National Collec-

tion of *Rodgersia*; woodland; herbaceous borders, and patio gardens with semi-hardy 'exotics'.

111 Pine Cottage Plants

Mr R. Fulcher, 1 Fourways, Eggesford EX18 7QZ
T: 01769 580076

Open: Jul, Aug, am, pm, except Sun, and under NGS

This small, plantsman's garden, contains a wealth of good ideas. Herbaceous perennials and shrubs form the background for a collection of over 200 varieties of *Agapanthus*. These are mostly in containers that come out for the summer, adding an exotic touch. Mr Fulcher also specializes in *Watsonia* and South African *Plectanthrus*, which are raised in his nursery tunnels. This garden holds the National Collection of *Agapanthus*.

112 St Merryn

Dr & Mrs W. Bradford, High Park Road, Braunton EX33 2LG
T: 01271 813805

Open: Under NGS, one Sun each in Apr, May, Jun, Jul, am, pm

A mature garden on the outskirts of Braunton, surrounded by trees, laid out in the 1930s with conifers, rhododen-

trees, the site was bare when John Smith came, but now the trees he planted in the 1980s are maturing there are shady areas, and secret corners. Acers and bamboos, ferns and grasses flourish here, and some areas of the garden have a marked oriental feel. A 'board walk' is planned for the perimeter and across a large bog area to allow closer inspection of native and exotic plants.

MID

114 Little Cumbre

Dr & Mrs J. Lloyd, Little Cumbre,
145 Pennsylvania Road, Exeter EX4 6DZ
T: 01392 258315

Open: Under NGS, some Sun Feb for snowdrops; some Sun, Apr–May

Situated high on the slopes above Exeter, this modern bungalow has wonderful views across the Exe valley and far beyond. To the front is a formal garden with borders, terracing, and many climbers – clematis is a feature in late spring. Behind the bungalow is woodland. There are about 30 varieties of snowdrops, for which the garden is now well known. The first were planted in the mid-1980s, when the present owners bought the property.

115 20 Monmouth Avenue

Mr & Mrs H. Lock, 20 Monmmouth Avenue,
Topsham EX3 0AF
T: 01392 873734

Open: By appt

Tall trees ensure privacy for this small garden (above left) in the heart of a residential area, and also create shade so that the effects of drought are less severe than might be expected on this site. The front area is planted as a scree bed, and to the rear are beds of hostas, pulmonarias, herbaceous perennials, and many

drons, camellias and palm trees. There are two small ponds – one with a Japanese influence. Herbaceous borders, one of which is devoted to delphiniums, give summer interest. The front garden is dominated by copper beeches, with formal beds edged with thrift and sedums.

113 The Water Garden

Mr J. Smith, Highcroft, Moorend, Wembworthy,
Chulmleigh EX18 7SG
T: 01837 83566

Open: By appt, and under NGS, Sat, Sun, end May–end Jul, pm

John Smith's garden is based on experience he gained as the owner of a specialist nursery. It is designed so that plants that like to grow in, or near to, water can be grown in their correct environments, and there are many unusual species on display. The site slopes, and is without a natural water source, so the ponds and cascades are all fed artificially. Over the years some of the larger ponds have become good wildlife habitats. But for two climbers. It is rich in good ideas for small spaces.

116 Rock House Gardens & Nursery

Mr & Mrs D. Boulton, Station Hill, Chudleigh TQ13 0EE
T: 01626 852134
Open: Daily except 25 Dec–1 Jan

In the shelter of Chudleigh Rock, a well-known viewpoint, is an unusual garden in a landscape created from limestone rocks. Some of the fine specimen trees – including ginkgo, black mulberry, maple, and mimosa – were planted when the house was built in the 19th century. Others have been added by the present owners, who have run their nursery here since 1946, when they took over the site (complete with Nissen huts) from American servicemen after the Second World War. There are interesting wildlife trails and walks to explore, and in autumn the ground is covered with cyclamen.

117 Wood Barton

Mr & Mrs R. Horton, Wood Barton, Kentisbeare, Cullompton EX15 2AT
T: 01884 266285
Open: By appt

A woodland garden of 0.8ha (2a) surrounds the beautiful Grade I manor house (right), which dates from the 14th century. When the owners came here as farmers in the 1970s, the tree canopy was already mature. Beneath it they have planted magnolias, rhododendrons, camellias, and drifts of daffodils. Groves of *Acers*, and some fine specimen trees, including a *Davidia*, a *Liriodendron*, a Judas tree, and several

walnuts, enhance the planting, and the autumn colours are lovely.

EAST

118 Lee Ford

Mr & Mrs N. Lindsay-Fynn, Lee Ford, Budeligh Salterton EX9 7AJ
T: 01395 445894; E: crescent@leeford.co.uk
Open: By appt

This delightful, small estate was originally a farm. The house is Queen Anne, with 18th- and 19th-century additions. The formal garden next to the house, much altered in the 1990s, contains an Adam pavilion looking out over lawns and herbaceous borders. The woodland gardens were developed in the 1950s, inspired by the Saville Gardens at Windsor, and contain camellias, rhododendrons, magnolias and azaleas. There is a hidden rose garden; a walled garden with fruit and vegetables, and a bog garden.

119 The Manor House

Mr & Mrs D. Campbell, The Manor House, Combpyne, Axminster EX13 8SX
T: 01297 445084
Open: Under NGS, one Sat, Sun, Jun, Sep

Dating in parts from the 13th century, it is thought that the Grade II manor house was once a nunnery, and that there has

the Alpine Garden Society his garden has filled with over 2,800 different specimens. Although there are a few large trees and shrubs, this intriguing garden is mostly devoted to miniatures. There are raised beds, and troughs made from polystyrene boxes, chicken wire, and tufa. Most of these have a life of about three years before they are emptied and replanted with stock grown from seed. Roger Stuckey propagates his alpines in the garden to the rear of the house, and many of the plants are for sale at very reasonable prices. Experts and enthusiasts will enjoy this garden, which is listed in the *RHS Plant Finder*.

121 Regency House
Mrs J. Parsons, Hemyock, Cullompton EX15 3RQ
T: 01823 680238; E: jenny.parsons@btinternet.com
Open: By appt

A tree-lined drive (below right) leads up to the 19th-century house with its courtyards and stables, which are still well used. Water flows down through the five-acre (2ha) gardens to feed a large pond at the bottom, and has been put to good use on its journey. There is a traditional walled garden, sloping lawns, and the atmosphere of a typical English country house.

122 Shrubbery Bungalow & Hortus Nursery
Mr & Mrs M. Houghton, Shrubbery Bungalow, School Lane, Rousdon DT7 3XW
T: 01297 444019; E: plants@hortusnursery.com;
www.hortusnursery.com
Open: 1 Mar–31 Oct, Wed–Sat, am, pm

A modern garden is being created to the rear of the bungalow and nursery, which has the accolade of supplying Chelsea

been some form of garden here for 800 years. The small church is next door, in a deep valley. This is a large garden on a steep hillside, managed for wildlife, and becoming increasingly 'natural' the higher it climbs, with wild flowers and bulbs taking over from the cultivated garden areas (above) immediately behind the house. Here the accent is on simple, cottage-style plants – pinks and foxgloves; rambling roses, irises and peonies – divided from the woodland by a medieval wall. There are four ponds, three with wild marsh plants in the damp soil, and one ancient pond near the house. The garden is a listed Medieval Site.

120 38 Phillipps Avenue
Mr & Mrs R.G. Stuckey, 38 Phillips Avenue, Exmouth EX8 3HZ
T: 01395 273636; E:stuckeysalpines@aol.com
Open: Under NGS, and by appt

Roger Stuckey started growing alpines as a hobby: since becoming a member of

Flower show and the Regents Park Flower Show. There is a maritime influence, with pebble-beds and driftwood, planted with grasses, herbs, interesting annuals, and plants that give colour from mid-summer onwards.

SOUTH

123 Hill House Nursery & Garden

Mr & Mrs R. Hubbard, Matthew Hubbard, Landscove, nr Ashburton TQ13 7LY
T: 01803 762273; F: 01803 762273; E: sacha@garden506.fsnet.co.uk; www.hillhousenursery.co.uk

Open: Daily, am, pm, except 15 Dec–9 Jan. No dogs

This former vicarage was owned by Edward Hyams, a well-known gardening author, who, between 1960 and 1968, created a fine garden here. By 1981, when the Hubbards moved in, little of the garden was left, but Hyams' book *An Englishman's Garden* helped with the restoration. There are many mature trees, and recently Hyams' Hydrangea Walk has been replanted with hydrangeas and camellias; many of the borders contain unusual plants. There is a pretty fish pond; a small greenhouse, and a duck pond surrounded by a living willow fence. The family-run nursery sells some 3,000 kinds of plants from the extensive glasshouses.

124 83 Mothecombe

Mr B. Newton, 83 Mothecombe, Holbeton, Plymouth PL8 1LB
T: 01752 830595

Open: as Mothecombe House (84)

The Head Gardener at **Mothecombe House** (84) moved to his present cottage in 2003, and was faced with the challenge of an overgrown plot. Having cleared the brambles and *Cupressus leylandii*, Bradley Newton could plan his irregular garden. He describes his planting schemes as abstract and informal, with an emphasis on colour. The overall effect is of a garden full of life, with succulents and sun-lovers revelling in the mild climate. Exotics, such as a banana and several cannas, grow alongside traditional herbs and rockery plants. The garden is still very much at the experimental stage, and future developments can be expected.

125 Paignton Zoo Environmental Park

Totnes Road, Paignton TQ4 7EU
T: 01803 697500; E: ian.turner@paigntonzoo.org.uk; www.paigntonzoo.org.uk.

Open: Daily, except 25 Dec, am, pm

Over 75 acres (30ha) (75a) of grounds are home to a wide range of birds, reptiles, and mammals, providing for them the most natural habitats possible. The zoo opened in 1923, and in the late 1950s became the world's first combined zoological and botanical gardens. Themed areas represent savannah, desert, wetland, and tropical forest, with tropical and desert glasshouses. There is plenty of water, and the whole site is well designed and

laid out. Over 20,000 plants, representing 2,500 different species, have been incorporated since 1997 – all designed to increase visitor interest, and improve life for the inhabitants.

126 Pleasant View

Mr & Mrs B.D. Yeo, Two Mile Oak, nr Denbury, Newton Abbot TQ12 6DG
T: 01803 813388

Open: Garden, May–Sep, Wed, Fri, pm; Nursery: mid-Mar–end Sep, Wed–Fri, am, pm

The National Collections of *Salvia* and *Abelia* are held here, and several beds and borders are devoted to these species. The nursery grows many rare and unusual shrubs, and in 1993 the adjoining field was developed to house a growing collection of shrubs and trees. There is also a buddleia avenue. Trees surround the gently sloping site, providing shelter, and broad grass paths pass between wide borders, full of the plants propagated and sold in the nursery. The gardens and arboretum cover an area of four acres (1.6ha).

127 1 Tipton Lodge

Angela Avis & Robin Pickering, 1 Tipton Lodge, Tipton St John, Sidmouth
T: 01404 813371

Open: Twice in Jun, and by appt May–Jun

Lying to one side of the Victorian house, the garden is shaded by mature trees. Roses feature in the formal herbaceous borders that form the backbone of this half-acre (0.2ha) garden. Vegetables are grown organically, and a fernery is developing under the trees. The tessellated tile floor of the former conservatory has been utilized as an outdoor garden room, with cast-iron fountains, ferns and pot plants.

DARTMOOR

128 Cleave House

Mr & Mrs R. Bowden, Cleave House, Sticklepath, Okehampton EX20 2NL
T: 01837 840481

Open: Apr, May, Jun, some Sat/Sun, am, pm, and by appt

The Bowdens' garden, which covers half an acre (0.2ha), is planted with some fine trees and shrubs, and is home to the National Collection of *Hosta*. An area to the back of the house is devoted to the species, and large beds are densely planted with huge clumps, which flourish in the dappled shade. In the adjoining nursery, 750 different varieties of *Hosta* are propagated.

129 Peveril Clematis Nursery

Mr & Mrs B. Fretwell, Village Road, Christow EX6 7NG
T: 01647 252937

Sheltered in the Teign valley is the nursery and garden of one of the leading experts on clematis, a man who has devoted himself to the cultivation, hybridization, and propagation of this popular climber. The garden is full of different varieties and species of clematis, and the house is covered with them. Growing alongside the clematis are numerous fine trees and shrubs, and the well-designed garden also has a stream and a pond.

Nurseries

The growth of garden centres in the 1990s brought about the demise of many small, traditionally run nurseries. The sale of plants was no longer left to professional horticulturists. Instead, mass-produced plants for both the garden and the house, often imported, became widely available in supermarkets, petrol stations, DIY stores, and many other retail outlets. It is encouraging to report a healthy swing back to small nurseries, propagating their own stock and imparting knowledgeable advice to their customers. Devon now has a good number of such concerns, and some very good specialists. Many of the smaller ones have limited openings, and limited stocks, so that a phone call is always advisable to save a wasted journey. Garden centres – many of which are very well worth a visit – are widely advertised, and range in size from enterprises covering several acres to agricultural merchants and corner-shops. These have not been included here.

Nurseries

Of the nurseries below, 26 are in the *RHS Plant Finder*. Those open to visitors are asterisked. The list is in two sections:

1 *Nurseries associated with the gardens in the Guide*, where further information will be found. Most gardens sell plants when they are open, but those listed are permanent nurseries, open to the public even when not visiting the garden. Among them, 'plant centres' are smaller than 'nurseries', which in some cases are substantial.

2 *Plant nurseries* not associated with gardens.

1 Nurseries associated with gardens

*Ann & Roger Bowden, Cleave House, Sticklepath, Okehampton EX20 2NL. T: 01837 840481. *Hostas.*

Burrow Farm Gardens, Old Taunton Road, Dalwood EX13 7ET. T: 01404 831285.

*Chapel Farm Nursery, Halwill Junction, Beaworthy EX21 5UF. T: 01409 221594.

Fast Rabbit Farm, Ash Cross, Dartmouth TQ6 0LR. T: 01803 712437.

*Feebers Hardy Plants, 1 Feebers Cottage, Broadclyst, Exeter EX5 3DQ. T: 01404 822118. *Plants for wet/clay soils.*

The Garden House, Buckland Monachorum, Yelverton PL20 7LQ.

Glebe Cottage Plants, Warkleigh, Umberleigh, EX37 9DH. T: 01769 540554. *Unusual perennials.*

*Hill House Nursery, Landscove, Ashburton TQ13 7LY. T: 01803 762273.

*Marwood Hill Gardens, Marwood, Barnstaple EX31 4EB. T: 01271 342528.

*Peveril Clematis Nursery, Village Road, Christow EX6 7NG. T: 01647 252937. *Clematis – species and hyrbids.*

Pine Cottage Plants, 1 Fourways, Eggesford EX18 7QZ. T: 01769 580076. *National Collection of Agapanthus.*

*Plant World Botanic Gardens, St Marychurch Road, Newton Abbot TQ12 4SE. T: 01803 872939.

*Pleasant View Nursery, Two Mile Oak, nr Denbury, Newton Abbot TQ12 6DG. T: 01803 813388. *National Collections of Salvia and Abelia.*

*Rowden Gardens, Brentor, Tavistock PL19 0NG. T: 01822 810275. *National Collections of Plygonum, Iris ensata, Caltha, and Ranunculus – all water plants.*

*Sampford Shrubs, Sampford Peverell, Tiverton EX16 7EN. T: 01884 821164. *National Collection of Heleniums. Organically raised shrubs, trees, perennials.*

*Sherwood Cottage, Newton St Cyres, Exeter EX5 5BT. T: 01392 851589. *National Collection of* Knaphill azaleas; *magnolias, hardy trees and shrubs.*

*Stone Lane Gardens, Stone Farm, Drewsteignton, Chagford TQ13 8JU. T: 01647 231311. *National Collections of alder and birch trees.*

*Stuckey's Alpines, 38 Phillipps Avenue, Exmouth EX8 3HZ. T: 01395 273636. *Wide variety of alpines.*

*Turnpike Cottage Plants, Trow, Salcombe Regis, Sidmouth EX10 0PB. T: 01395 515265. Echiums – *seeds of large number of herbaceous perennials and rock plants.*

*Ward Alpines, Newton Farm, Hemyock, Cullompton EX15 3QS. T: 01823 680410. *National Collections of* Gentians *and* Rhodohypoxis; *also* Iris ensata *and* I. siberica.

*Nigel Wright Rhododendrons, The Old Glebe, Eggesford, EX18 7QU. T: 01769 580632. *By appointment only. Rhododendrons.*

2 Plant nurseries

Note: Nurseries listed without postcodes do not usually trade by mail order.

Ash Moor Nursery, Rose Ash, South Molton EX36 4RF. T: 01884 860355.

*The Big Grass Co., Hookhill Plantation, Woofardisworthy, nr Crediton EX17 4RX. T: 01363 866146. *Grasses.*

Blyth's Devon Nurseries, Exeter Road, Dawlish. T: 01626 863131.

*Bramley Lodge Nursery, Beech Tree Lane, Ipplepen, Newton Abbot TQ12 5TW. T: 01803 813265. *Grasses, trees and shrubs, with themed display areas.*

Broad Oak Nursery, Mowlish Lane, Kenton. T: 01626 890034.

*Burnham Nurseries (Orchid Paradise), Forches Cross, Newton Abbott TQ12 6PZ. T: 01626 352233.

*Cottage Garden Plants & Herbs, North Lodge, Canonteign, Christow EX6 7NS. T: 01647 252950. *Hardy geraniums.*

*Devon Violet Nursery, Rattery, South Brent TQ10 5BQ. T: 01364 643033. *National Collection of* Viola odorata.

Dolton Nursery, Brook Road, Dolton. T: 01805 603618.

Donhatch Nursery, Combe Raleigh, Honiton EX14 4TQ. T: 01404 42981.

*Dulford Nursery, Cullompton EX15 2DG. T: 01884 266361. *Native trees and shrubs.*

Charles Dumpelton, Town Barton, Highampton, Beaworthy EX21 5LE. T: 01409 231302.

*Endsleigh Gardens, Tavistock PL29 0PG. T: 01822 870235. *Unusual trees and shrubs; old varieties apples and cherries.*

*Fairhaven Nursery, Clapworthy Cross, Chittlehampton, Umberleigh EX37 9QT. 01769 540528. *Unusual hardy trees and shrubs.*

*Fernwood Nursery, Fernwood, Petersmarland, Torrington EX38 8QG. T: 01805 601446. *National Collection of* Sempervivum, Jovarbia, Rosularia, *and* Phormium.

*Fillans Plants, Tuckermarsh Gardens, Tamar Lane, Bere Alston PL20 7HN. T: 01822 840721. *Bamboos, hydrangeas, unusual woody plants.*

*Hidden Valley Nursery, Umberleigh EX37 9BUT: 01769 560567. *Hardy perennials, especially shade-lovers.*

Jack's Patch, Coles Barn, Newton Road, Bishopsteignton, Teignmouth. T: 01626 776996.

*Kenwith Nursery, Blinsham, Torrington EX19 8NT. T: 01805 603 274. *National Collection of dwarf conifers.*

*Lydford Alpine Nursery, 2 Southern Cottages, Lydford EX20 4BL. T: 01822 820398. Saxifrage *and unusual alpines.*

M.G.M. Nurseries, Woolston Lodge, Loddiswell, Kingsbridge. T: 01548 550754.

*M & M Plants, Lloret, Chittlehampton, Umberleigh EX37 9PD. T: 01769 540448. *Perennials, trees and shrubs.*

Marsh Broadmoor Nusery, Exmouth Road, Ottery St Mary. T: 01404 822738.

*Meadow Cottage Plants, Pitt Hill, Ivybridge PL21 0JJ. T: 01752 894532. *Hardy geraniums, bamboos and grasses.*

Merry Harriers, Woolsery, Bideford EX39 5QH . T: 01237 431611.

*Nicky's Rock Garden Nursery, Broadhayes, Stockland, Honiton EX14 9EH. T: 01404 881213. *Plants for scree, troughs, rockery, dwarf shrubs.*

*Otter Nurseries Ltd., Gosford Road, Ottery St Mary EX11 1LZ. T: 01404 815815.

*The Palm House, 8 North St, Ottery St Mary EX11 1DR. T: 01404 815450. *Palms.*

*Pounsley Plants, Pounsley Combe, Spridlestone, Brixton. PL9 0DW. T: 01752 402873. *Old roses, clematis, herbaceous perennials.*

Rock Nursery, Station Hill, Chudleigh. T: 01626 852134.

Ron Tucker, Halsewood Farm, Cullompton. T: 01884 32486.

*Rosedown Mill, Hartland, Bideford EX39 6AH. T: 01237 441527. *Palms, cyciades, pachypodiums.*

*St Bridgets Nurseries Ltd., Old Rydon Lane, Exeter EX2 7JY. T: 01395 873672.

*Silver Dale Nurseries, Shute Lane, Combe Martin, Barnstaple EX34 0HT. T: 01271 882539. *National Collection of Fuchsia; hardy fuchsias.*

*South West Carnivorous Plants, 2 Rose Cottage, Culmstock, Cullompton EX15 3JJ. T: 01884 841549. *Carniverous plants.*

Tarhan Nursery, Shiphay Nursery, Colyton EX24 6EU. T: 01297 553570.

Teign Valley Nursery, Bridford Mill, Bridford. T: 01647 252654.

Thorndon Cross Nursery, Whincote, Thorndon Cross, Okehamtpon EX20 4NF. T: 018137 861347.

*Thornhayes Nursery, St Andrews Wood, Dulford, Cullompton EX15 2DF. T: 01884 266746. *Fruit trees, especially Westcountry varieties of apple.*

*Westcountry Lupins, Ford Hill Forge, Hartland, Bideford EX39 6EE. T: 01237 441208. *Lupins, lewisias, hellebores, gentians, lavender, grasses.*

Withleigh Nurseries, Withleigh, Tiverton EX16 8JG. T: 01884 253351.

Calendar of Garden Openings

1 Gardens open all year

Bicton College Gardens & Arboretum (53)
Bicton Park Botanical Gardens (54)
Castle Drogo (91)
Cockington Court (72)
Dartington Hall Gardens (75)
Escot Fantasy Gardens (59)
Killerton Gardens (42)
Mair & Thompson at Flete Walled Gardens (83)
Marwood Hill (29)
Overbecks (85)

Paignton Zoo Environmental Park (125)
RHS Garden Rosemoor (32)
Sherwood (48)

2 Gardens open on a regular basis

Arlington Court (13)
Blackpool Gardens (70)
Buckland Abbey (2)
Burrow Farm Gardens (56)
Cliffe (17)
Coleton Fishacre (73)
Docton Mill (19)
Endsleigh (4)
Fast Rabbit Farm (76)
The Garden House (5)
Glebe Cottage (22)
Greenway (77)
Hartland Abbey (24)
Hill House Nursery & Garden (123)
Knightshayes Gardens (43)
Lewtrenchard Manor (6)
Mythic Garden (98)
Peco Gardens (66)
38 Phillipps Avenue (120)
Plant World (86)
Powderham Castle (47)
Rock House Gardens & Nursery (116)
Saltram House (10)
Tapeley Park (35)
Winsford Walled Garden (37)
Yonder Hill (69)

3 Gardens open only occasionally

February
Little Cumbre (114)
Knightshayes Gardens (43)

March
Dippers (93)
Fast Rabbit Farm (76)
Glebe Cottage (22)
Heathercombe Woodland Garden (95)
Higher Knowle (96)
Lukesland (97)

Mothecombe House (84)
Westcott Barton (36)
Wood Barton (117)

April
Andrew's Corner (88)
Bickham House (38)
Bishops Palace, *see* page 7
Castle Hill (15)
Chapel Farm House (108)
Cleave House (128)
Dippers (93)
The Downes (20)
Gorwell House (23)
Haldon Grange (39)
Heathercombe Woodland Garden (95)
Higher Knowle (96)
Holbrook Garden (40)
Kia-Ora Farm (41)
Lukesland (97)
Little Cumbre (114)
The Moorings (63)
Mothecombe House (84)
83 Mothecombe (124)
Newton Farm (45)
Shobrooke Park Gardens (49)
Southcombe House (100)
Spillifords Wildlife Garden (50)
Westcott Barton (36)

May
Alswood (12)
Andrew's Corner (88)
Bickham House (38)
Castle Hill (15)
Cherubeer Gardens (16)
Churchpark Cottage (71)
The Cider House (3)
Cleave House (128)
Dicot (58)
The Downes (20)
Durcombe Water (21)
Gorwell House (23)
Haldon Grange (39)
Hamblyn's Coombe (78)

Heathercombe Woodland Garden (95)
Higher Knowle (96)
Holbrook Garden (40)
Inglewood (81)
Kia-Ora Farm (41)
Kingston House (82)
The Lodge (7)
Lukesland (97)
Milland Farm (30)
The Moorings (63)
Mothecombe House (84)
83 Mothecombe (124)
Newton Farm (45)
The Old Garden (64)
Pikes Cottage (46)
Shobrooke Park Gardens (49)
Southcombe House (100)
Sowton Mill (101)
Spillifords Wildlife Garden (50)
Sutton Mead (102)
Taikoo (103)
Westscott Barton (36)
Whitstone Farm (104)
Wrangaton House (105)

June

The African Garden (1)
Alswood (12)
Andrew's Corner (88)
Barleycott (14)
Bickham House (38)
Bovey Tracey Gardens (90)
Bundels (55)
Castle Hill (15)
The Cider House (3)
Cherubeer Gardens (16)
The Croft (18)
Dicot (58)
Dippers (93)
The Downes (20)
Drury Head Cottage (94)
Durcombe Water (21)
Gorwell House (23)
Heathercombe Woodland Garden (95)
Heddon Hall (25)

High Barn (79)
Higher Knowle (96)
Holbrook Garden (40)
Inglewood (81)
Kerscott House (27)
Kia-Ora Farm (41)
Kingston House (82)
The Lodge (7)
Little Webbery & Little Webbery Cottage (28)
Kerscott House (27)
Milland Farm (30)
Mothecombe House (84)
83 Mothecombe (124)
Newton Farm (45)
The Old Garden (64)
Pikes Cottage (46)
Portington (9)
School House (33)
Scypen (87)
Shapcott Barton Estate (34)
Shobrooke Park Gardens (49)
Southcombe House (100)
Spillifords Wildlife Garden (50)
Taikoo (103)
Ways Cottage (68)
Weighbridge Lodge (11)
Westcott Barton (36)

July

The African Garden (1)
Alswood (12)
Andrew's Corner (88)
Bickham House (38)
Blackhall Manor (89)
Cadhay (57)
Chapel Farm House (108)
Cherubeer Gardens (16)
The Croft (18)
Dicot (58)
The Downes (20)
Drury Head Cottage (94)
Gorwell House (23)
High Barn (79)
Holbrook Garden (40)

Hole Farm (80)
Inglewood (81)
Kerscott (27)
Kia-Ora Farm (41)
Kingston House (82)
Little Ash Farm (62)
Little Webbery (28)
The Lodge (7)
Milland Farm (30)
Mothecombe House (84)
83 Mothecombe (124)
Newton Farm (45)
Paddocks (65)
Pikes Cottage (46)
School House (33)
Shapcott Barton Estate (34)
Taw Bank (89)
Taw Meadow (89)
Sowton Mill (101)
Spillifords Wildlife Garden (50)
Ways Cottage (68)
Weighbridge Lodge (11)
Westcott Barton (36)
Ugbrooke Park (51)

August
The African Garden (1)
Alswood (12)
Bickham House (38)
Cadhay (57)
Chapel Farm House (108)
The Croft (18)
Durcombe Water (21)
Holbrook Garden (40)
Kerscott House (27)
Kia-Ora Farm (41)
Little Ash Farm (62)
Milland Farm (30)
Newton Farm (45)
Pikes Cottage (46)
Shapcott Barton Estate (34)
Spillifords Wildlife Garden (50)
Weighbridge Lodge (11)
Westcott Barton (36)
Ugbrooke Park (51)

September
Bickham House (38)
Castle Farm (92)
The Cider House (3)
Gorwell House (23)
Holbrook Garden (40)
Kia-Ora Farm (41)
Newton Farm (45)
Pikes Cottage (46)
Whitstone Farm (104)
Ugbrooke Park (51)

October
Gorwell House (23)
Pikes Cottage (46)

2   Gardens open by appointment only
Collepardo (74)
1 Feebers Cottage (60)
Higher Watertown (26)
Jasmine Cottage (61)
The Old Glebe (31)
Longham (8)
Little Southey (44)
Sutton Mead (102)
Rowden Gardens (99)
Turnpike Cottage (61)
Withleigh Farm (52)

Index

Acknowledgements

Photographs are reproduced by kind permission of: Heidi Amschwand, pp. 90, 91; Kenneth Ashburner, pp. 222, 223; Sharon Bailey, p. 49 (B); John & Julia Barton, p. 79 (TR, B); John & Lana Borrett, pp. 56, 57; R.A. Bracey, pp. 198, 199; Katie Bunn, p. 235 (T); D. Campbell, p. 242; Devon Tourism, p. 11; Jessica Duncan, p. 73 (T); The English Riviera Tourist Board, p. 13 (T); Kate Foster, pp. 168, 169; Veronica Gilbert, pp. 52, 53; Dr G. Haig, pp. 120, 121; Alison Hodge, pp. 82, 83 (B), 149 (B); James Hodge, pp. 16–17, 114, 162–3; Christopher Laughton, p. 2; Freya Laughton, pp. 126–7; Dr J.A. Marston, pp. 64, 65 (B); Bridget McCrum, p. 181; The National Trust, pp. 44, 104, 105 (T); The National Trust/John Bethell, p. 107 (B), cover; The National Trust/ Steve Bond, pp. 178, 179; The National Trust/Peter Cade, p.171; The National Trust/Alec MacKenzie, p.170; The National Trust/John Melville, p. 45 (T); The National Trust/Phil Rider, p. 105 (B); The National Trust/Sally Whitfield, pp. 20, 21; Powderham Estate Office, p. 115; Diane Rowe, pp. 108, 109; Dr J. Shelley, pp. 15, 118; Philip Smith, pp. 140, 141; Lady Angela Stucley, pp. 7; 66–7; Mr R. Thistlethwayte, pp.136–7; Mr & Mrs J. Tremlett, p. 97 (T). All other photographs are by the author.

The map inside the back cover is © Collins Bartholomew Ltd 2004 Reproduced by permission of HarperCollins Publishers.

Garden Visit Notes